Nigel Bromage was commissioned into the Grenadier Guards in 1945 at the age of seventeen. In 1947 he was seconded to the Arab Legion and fought with them at the Battle of Latroun in 1948. He stayed with the Arab Legion until 1955 and then became Assistant Military Attaché in the British Embassy in Amman until 1961. In 1963 Bromage was sent to Saudi Arabia to set up the British Military Mission to the Saudi Arabian National Guard (SANG), under the newly appointed commander, Prince Abdullah bin Abdul Aziz. He received an OBE for his work with SANG and stayed in the Arabian Peninsula for most of the rest of his service, first as an adviser to the Kuwait Liaison Team and finally as Military Adviser to the British Embassy in the UAE. He retired in 1978. Over the years, he has played an integral role in Saudi–British relations.

Sir Alan Munro was British Ambassador in Saudi Arabia 1989–1993 and Under-Secretary of State for the Middle East and Africa.

For my beloved wife

Without whose energy and drive this memoir
would never have been published

A SOLDIER IN ARABIA

A British Military Memoir from Jordan to Saudi Arabia

Nigel Bromage

with an Introduction by Sir Alan Munro

The Radcliffe Press

LONDON • NEW YORK

Published in 2012 by Radcliffe Press
An imprint of I.B.Tauris & Co. Ltd
6 Salem Road, London W2 4BU
175 Fifth Avenue, New York NY 10010
www.ibtauris.com

Distributed in the United States and Canada Exclusively by
Palgrave Macmillan,
175 Fifth Avenue, New York NY 10010

ISBN 978 1 78076 082 7

A full CIP record for this book is available from the British Library
A full CIP record for this book is available from the Library of Congress
Library of Congress catalog card: available

Typeset in Calisto by Dexter Haven Associates Ltd, London
Printed and bound by CPI Group (UK) Ltd, Croydon, CR0 4YY

Contents

List of Illustrations

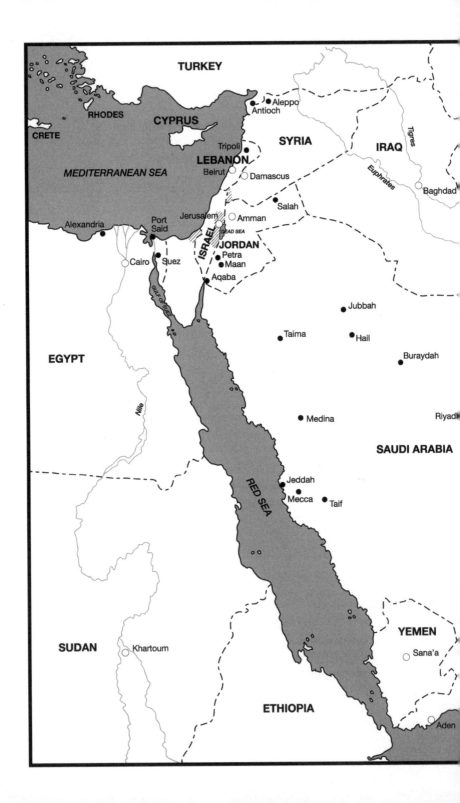

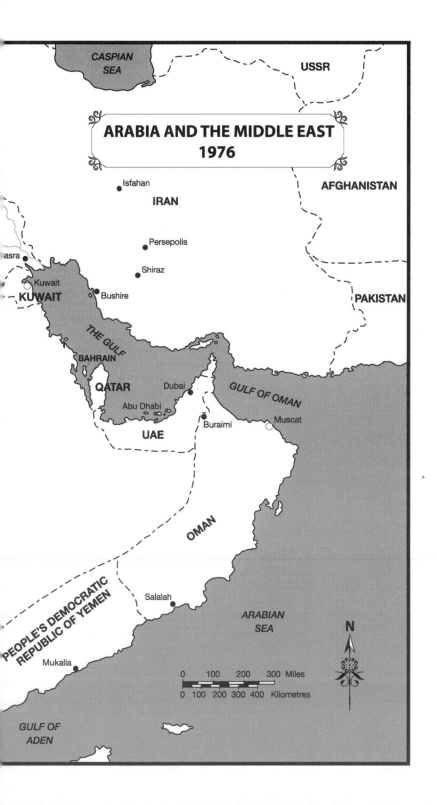

Preface

My life in Jordan and in Palestine was shaped by the emergence of the state of Israel. It had an uneasy birth, starting with a wave of terrorism before and after the Second World War. Israelis can be assertive and hold out for their right to exist in an unaccommodating era. This has resulted in their being regarded by some as an enemy of the Arab people of Jordan and Jerusalem, and even to many in the outside world.

When I first went to Jordan, King Abdullah bin Hussein had emerged as a founder of the Hashemite Dynasty in that country. There followed a time when the pressure in Jerusalem had forced the notables of that city to ask King Abdullah to check the takeover by the Israelis of the area of the Old City of Jerusalem. As a result, units of the Jordanian Army became deeply involved in the struggle for control of the Old City. The Jordanian Army was successful in defending the rights of the Muslim population of the New City and resisting Israeli pressure. Eventually a status quo was reached in which a limited area of the Old City of Jerusalem came under Jordanian control. This has pertained since that time. Outside Jerusalem, in the country of Palestine, the Israelis persisted in trying to assert their dominance over the local Arab community. Many battles between the Israelis, now incorporated, through the influence of the United States, into a state of Israel, continued to take place all over the northern part of Jordan. There followed a wave of treaties between the states of Israel and Jordan. Many small battles were fought by Jordanians and Palestinians to keep the two sides from each other's throats. In this turmoil, I have never had any bias in favouring of one side or the other, but have done my best to keep an uneasy peace between them.

Acknowledgements

I am most grateful to the following people, without whose help and guidance my memoir would not have been written. Sir Alan Munro for his advice and for writing the Introduction. Linda and Laurence Kelly for their literary advice. Bessam al Zaim. The Cayzer Trust Company Limited for their assistance with print-outs before publication. Dr Lester Crook for all his help and patience in editing. Lastly, and by no means least, Pamela Stone for all her hard work and help in typing the manuscript. I am eternally grateful to her.

Introduction

Sir Alan Munro

The last century produced a notable roll-call of British military officers who chose to make their careers amid the political upheavals of the Middle East, as the tribal dynasties and the merchant societies of this vast region of sands and highlands sought to carve new destinies for themselves out of the legacies of Ottoman and subsequent European tutelage. For some of these individuals it was the call of adventure that held a strong appeal; for many it was the lure of irregular warfare in command of warriors whose traditional allegiances to tribe and to territory amid an often testing environment appealed to an irresistible romantic strain. The majority among them absorbed a deep familiarity with the cultures and the systems of the Arab societies among which they lived, and a lasting trust and affection which they found to be warmly reciprocated. The diversity of rivalries and aspirations that motivated their new partners they soon made their own, albeit occasionally at odds with an imperial authority back in Britain to which they owed their commissions.

There are those among this gallery whose names have acquired particular resonance: Captain William Shakespeare, whose service to the Emir Abdul Aziz al Saud in central Arabia in his tribal tussles with the Ottoman-backed al Rashid during World War I was cut short when he was picked off in mid-battle while directing the fire of the Emir's field guns; Col. T.E. Lawrence, archaeologist turned soldier, whose dashing, if self-promoting, exploits in support of the British-sponsored tribal campaign by the Emir Faisal of the Hejaz to drive the Turks out of the deserts of eastern Arabia and Jordan have become the stuff of legend; General John Glubb Pasha, whose effective command of Transjordan's Bedouin Arab Legion during the ill-directed Arab contest with a nascent Israel in the late 1940s is well recorded in this memoir.

There were others, like Col. Harold Dickson, who turned from a military career to a lifetime in the Arab world engaged in the establishment of effective administration among the tribes of southern Iraq and of Kuwait under the benevolent aegis of a dominant Pax Britannica; and Col. Ronald Storrs, a classical scholar and key member of the Arab Bureau in Cairo during World War I, who went on to be Governor of Jerusalem during the fraught years of early Jewish immigration into Palestine, and then of Cyprus. Nor was this deep involvement in the Middle East affairs entirely one-sided. The Zionist cause found its champion in Orde Wingate. Son of a

Military Governor of the Sudan, here was an inspirational if erratic army officer who took upon himself the creation in Palestine in the 1930s, under indulgent British eyes, of Jewish commando units; these would become the forerunners of the notorious Haganah underground force that would in due course undermine Britain's will to sustain her mandate over Palestine's intractable intercommunal conflict.

With his adventurous career, dedicated to the military endeavours and the security of those among whom he worked and lived for over thirty years across the Arab world from Jordan through Saudi Arabia to the emirates of the Gulf, Nigel Bromage merits his place among these champions. His memoir opens with lively accounts of personal involvement as a young commander of a Jordanian armoured unit in a variety of brushes with Israeli forces during the disastrous campaign which a divided Arab coalition alliance fought to resist Israeli occupation of Arab territory in the conflict which accompanied the birth of the state of Israel in May 1948. Only the Arab Legion, to which Bromage was seconded, gave a respectable account of itself, by holding on to the Old City of Jerusalem and other lands around the Dead Sea. The author's appetite for independent responsibility and improvisation, which would last throughout his unorthodox career, and earn the friendship and respect of his tribe of Arab friends, comes through clearly in these early military skirmishes. They present a contrast to the ceremonial routine of a guardsman's London duties, which was never to the taste of Nigel Bromage – nor perhaps unremarked by his immediate superiors.

The accounts of subsequent spells of dedicated involvement with the formation of competent security forces within the countries of Arabia, starting with the establishment in the 1960s under the present King Abdullah of Saudi Arabia's National Guard, and moving on to Kuwait and then the newly independent sheikhdoms which now form the United Arab Emirates, present a fascinating reminder, to those who today enjoy the modern amenities and air-conditioned comforts of existence in Arabia, of the more primitive yet companionable environment in which their expatriate predecessors found themselves, and their wives and families too. Nigel and Pamela Bromage adapted readily to life amid Arabia's devout culture with a relish that speaks for itself. The remarkable knowledge they acquired of the traditions, and the prejudices, of the Bedouin tribes among which they found themselves is mingled with their enthusiasm for desert wandering, and for the game-hunting expeditions which those less-policed times still allowed.

It was indeed the desert that first brought me into contact with Nigel Bromage. Turning up in Amman back in 1959 as a raw language student from the Foreign Office's Arabic Academy in Lebanon (popularly known in Arab circles as the School for Spies), Nigel, who was Military Attaché at the time, took me under his wing. I promptly found myself despatched, complete with Land Rover and Arab Legion driver plus a sheaf of British Army maps of largely unmapped desert, to undertake a search for isolated Howeitat Bedouin encampments in the sands and mountains of southern Jordan, where a food-relief operation was to be mounted following prolonged drought. It was not only an unforgettable experience, but also one that afforded more than a first glimpse of that fascination with the Arab world and its ways that has inspired this very personal memoir by 'A Soldier in Arabia'.

1

My Early Life

I was born at Ootacamund, India, on 14 April 1927. My father was an officer in the Indian Police who married my mother as his second wife. She was the daughter of Thomas Hawksley, a well-known and well-respected Victorian water engineer. They had met in the Channel Islands when my father was on leave, and to where my mother used to come regularly with her family.

Father had joined the Indian Police as there was not much money available. When he had passed the Civil Service Examination, the Indian Police offered paid employment at an early stage in his life. Father had been married before and had four children, so when he married mother I had two half-brothers and two half-sisters. One of my half-brothers entered the Colonial Service and was a resident in Nigeria. My other half-brother, John, entered the Navy through Dartmouth and commanded a submarine, with distinction, throughout the

Second World War. My half-sisters, at the beginning, used to look after me, standing in for nanny when she was on holiday.

In 1929, the family moved back to England and father bought a house and small estate in Herefordshire, called Dunfield, near Kington. We settled happily at Dunfield House. It subsequently turned out that my full brother was an epileptic and had to have special treatment throughout his early life. My mother and her mother, Mrs Hawksley, had been converted to Roman Catholicism before my father married her. Grandmother lived at a house called Thorpe Hall near Barnard Castle, close to the Scottish border. Father was Captain of the Kington Cricket Club. He was no great cricketer himself, but he employed a certain Sydney Barnes to teach my brother and I cricket. Sydney Barnes was a well-known cricketer who bowled medium pace leg-breaks and was selected to play for England for a number of years. As well as teaching us cricket, during his visit he played with the Kington cricket team, to which he was a great asset.

I was sent to a preparatory school called St Richard's in Little Malvern. The Headmaster was a Mr Keeble, and another master, a Mr Croft, had been at Ampleforth College. I was sent to Ampleforth by my parents. It was a long way from Herefordshire, so I used to travel there and back by train. I was at Ampleforth at the outbreak of the Second World War, and once I had passed my school certificate, I enlisted in the Grenadier Guards in which my uncle, Thomas Hawksley, had been a junior officer before me. In those days, at least one battalion of the Grenadier Guards was in the North Yorkshire area, adjacent to Ampleforth, so it was natural for me to follow into the Regiment.

I was keen to start soldiering before the war ended. My first appointment was as an officer cadet. I would have gone to Caterham, but the guards' depot was hit by a flying bomb towards the end of the war, so the young officer training was undertaken by the 1st Battalion Welsh Guards, which was then at Sandown Park, where it occupied the totes at the Racecourse. When I joined, I came under the tuition of a trained soldier who oversaw the early training of the new officer cadets. He was a great help to me in getting me through the various stages of an embryo career. From Sandown Park, I went to the Scots Guards, then at Pirbright in Surrey, from where I graduated as an officer cadet and passed out as a junior officer. I was eventually destined to go to Palestine with the 3rd Battalion Grenadier Guards.

2

The Beginning, from 1945

In January 1945, I joined the Training Battalion Grenadier Guards at Windsor. The only remarkable thing during that period was that I was asked to take part in an audition to sing with the two Princesses. This was an unhappy time, as the audition proved that my voice was so awful that I was turned out immediately. I have never sung in Church again, and I never shall.

When we were at the Training Battalion, it was decided that we were, as a draft, to go to the 3rd Battalion Grenadier Guards, then in Palestine. My closest companion in the Regiment was Robin Balniel, now Lord Crawford and Balcarres, who had joined directly from Eton, and we were both to go. (Apart from mentioning Robin Balniel, I do not refer to my brother officers or acquaintances by name in these memoirs.)

In those days, the normal route to Palestine was via a system called MEDLOCK. Like so many Army abbreviations,

The author (top row, second from left) in the Brigade Squad at Sandown Park in 1945.

I never discovered what MEDLOCK actually meant. However, what it meant, in fact, was that we travelled across France in dilapidated railway coaches, all of which had seen better days, to arrive at Hyères, which is just to the north of Toulon. From Hyères we took ship to Port Said, where we disembarked at a transit camp, which was commanded by Brigadier Sir Michael Dylwyn-Venables-Llewellyn, whom I had known from my days in Radnorshire. I do not know how he came to command a transit camp in Egypt, but I suspected that he had fallen foul of General Sir Allan Adair when the latter was commanding the Guards Division in Europe.

From Hyères we took ship to Port Said, from where we travelled by train to Cairo. Robin Balniel, the elder son of the Earl of Crawford and Balcarres, had discovered that a member of his family was involved in a Government Commission to discuss the future of Palestine.

When we reached Cairo, we took a taxi to the Mina House Hotel where we understood the Palestine Commission was in residence. On arriving at the Mina House, I shook hands with the Nubian door attendant and asked for the Palestine Commission. He answered immediately, 'In the bar, Sir.' I remember first meeting Richard Crossman there, who, in subsequent years, I came to know very well and dislike. Some years later, when a minister, he wrote his famous diaries, the publication of which caused such an outcry in the Labour Party.

Soon after reaching Palestine, we joined the 3rd Battalion Grenadier Guards, which was located north of Haifa, outside a village called Nahariya. When we reached Nahariya, we discovered that a ship with Israeli immigrants had recently beached there and the immigrants had dispersed, or gone to ground, somewhere in the neighbourhood. I was astonished by the Israeli settlers. The only Israelis I had met, before then, were distinguished by their gentle manners and religious bearing. As in all such internal security exercises, the 3rd Battalion was hampered by the difficulties of moving troops without being seen and reported upon by local dissidents.

We soldiered on in the 3rd Battalion until the summer months, when it was decided that it should take part in exercises in Transjordan, to which we moved in our own transport, towards the end of the summer. When we were in Transjordan, I was told that I was to be extra-regimentally employed, setting up a training camp for what was to be called the Supernumerary Palestine Police, just outside Ramle. I duly reported to the camp, which was commanded by an officer from the Transjordan Frontier Force called Sam Whitfield. Under his command were a number of non-commissioned officers, from various regiments, who were to train the Supernumerary Palestine Police. Also on his staff was an Inspector of Police called Leonard Board. We had great difficulty in getting suitable non-commissioned officers, as commanding officers were at pains to ensure that only inefficient non-commissioned officers were sent to the Supernumerary Palestine Police Depot, so training facilities were abysmal.

It turned out that Sam Whitfield had been a rough rider in one of the Household Cavalry regiments and his main aim in life was to enjoy himself. He took with him his mount, and he had hunted twice every week with the Ramle Vale Hounds. When I reached the training camp and saw the situation, I managed to get through on the telephone to my mother to ask her for the money to buy myself a horse. Money was not easily transferable without special Treasury authority, which she managed to obtain. I was able to buy a likely uncut colt of an iron-grey colour; he looked like one of my mother's Arab horses, but his Roman nose betrayed Australian blood in his ancestry. The Australian cavalry had turned out all their horses after the First World War, which sadly had contaminated the local Arabs, of which my new horse was quite clearly one. Leonard Board managed to produce a mare, I suspected by squeezing the arm of one of the local farmers, which in his capacity as a Palestine policeman he well could do. Sam had two German Shepherd dogs, one called Rex and a puppy called Blacky, which were his constant companions. One day, in the evening, we left the camp. Sam took with him a litter of Boxer puppies. When we were a mile and a half from our camp, we heard some shooting in the woods, very near us. Sam said to me, 'Nigel, would you look after the puppies while I go and see what it is?' He and Leonard Board rode across to the wood, from whence the shooting came. After a bit, there were a few more shots. That was the last we saw of them. I rode up to find out what had happened, and found Sam Whitfield dead and Leonard Board very seriously injured. We took him by truck to the local RAF Regiment clinic, which was very near, but he died that night. His last words to me were, 'Nigel, what have I done to deserve this?' I thought that the Israelis must have been in ambush, and had probably been watching our routine on a daily basis. We buried Sam and Leonard Board in the military cemetery at Ramle. Brigadier Johnson, who was then commanding Sarafand Camp, asked me to join him on a trip to Aqaba, which he had arranged in order, presumably, to give me a change of scenery after the disaster, but I suspect it was a 'jolly' which he had had in mind for some time, but had needed our transport in which to do it.

On our return from Aqaba, I discovered that the 1st Battalion Grenadier Guards had relieved the 3rd Battalion. The 1st Battalion headquarters was by then stationed at

Lydda Airport, where I duly joined it. The 1st Battalion had a new Commanding Officer who was disliked by his company commanders, because he objected to them playing poker with the Quartermaster. Just before I returned, the Commanding Officer was furious because various officers had formed a poker school and were busy playing poker with the Quartermaster and the local Palestine Police Commander, when the Commanding Officer walked in. The Quartermaster had become well off from illicitly cashing officers' cheques in Germany, at the end of the War, so no one minded taking some of his money back in poker games.

Things deteriorated under the new Commanding Officer to a degree whereby many of the officers were in favour of leaving the Battalion. In my case, another officer of about my seniority as a Captain and I, looked at a round robin exhortation from Headquarters Palestine for volunteers to join the Arab Legion. My friend and I at once volunteered, and were summoned to Amman to be introduced to Glubb Pasha. Transport was duly sent to Amman to convey our belongings and us across the Jordan Valley to meet the great man, in person. We were received by Brigadier Broadhurst, who was the Pasha's assistant and who had been from the Palestine Police. We were accepted into the Arab Legion and posted to various regiments of the Legion which were in Palestine. In my case, it was the 2nd Regiment, which at that time was stationed at Televinsky Camp, just outside Tel Aviv.

We duly re-crossed the Jordan Valley into Palestine. The Commanding Officer of the 2nd Arab Legion Regiment was a well-known figure from the Welsh Guards called Teal Ashton. He had acquired the nickname Teal as he was reputed to have been quick off the water.

At that point King Abdullah was under acute pressure to aid the inhabitants of Jerusalem, who were being besieged by the Israelis, who I believed had no intention of obeying any United Nations plea to cease military activity in the Holy City. The Arab Legion Forces, then available for the relief of Jerusalem, were 1st, 2nd and 3rd Regiments. The 1st Regiment was commanded by Ski Galetly, the 2nd Regiment by Lt Colonel Slade of the Suffolk Regiment, and the 3rd Regiment by a tough down-to-earth Australian called Newman. The Divisional Commander was a contract officer named Norman Lash, who had established his headquarters at Ramallah. When King Abdullah finally decided to relieve the remaining Arabs in Jerusalem he had, as his available forces, the 2nd Regiment, the 3rd Regiment, which was then in Northern Palestine, and the 4th Regiment, which was newly formed from various garrison companies, which Transjordan had raised in the country. The 2nd Regiment entered Jerusalem from the area of Sheikh Jerrah, in the north. Lt Colonel Slade, the Commanding Officer, was wounded by shrapnel, in his back, and was out of the fighting almost immediately. The problem was that the Hadasa Hospital and its compound blocked the entrance to the north of Jerusalem, and the 2nd Regiment had to fight hard in order to capture its immediate objectives. It was followed by the 3rd Regiment, which also took heavy casualties and was finally thwarted by being

Mohamed Khalouf, doctor to the 2nd Regiment.

unable to enter the Monastery of Notre Dame in the centre of the New City. In the end, the Legion was left in possession of the Old City. It was decided to extend the Legion to include a new 4th Regiment, a 5th Regiment on the de facto border between the Old City and the New, and a 6th Regiment to defend the walls of the Old City after it was captured. The 1st and 3rd Regiments were incorporated into the 1st Arab Legion Brigade under the command of Ski Galetly.

I have often been asked how I was able to speak good colloquial Arabic. I think the reasons are that my ear is in some way well attuned to the Arabic language, and I spent many years speaking only Arabic and no English, so the language came to me very easily. I read Arabic, without difficulty, but my written Arabic is weak, so I use it as little as possible.

3

The End of the Mandate, 1948

The Israelis had attacked at Jerusalem trying to seize as much as they could of the Old City and a large part of the New. The background to all this is contained in Sir John Glubb's book *The Story of the Arab Legion*. The fighting in Jerusalem was intense. The 2nd Regiment lost two commanding officers wounded in the battle. The Arab Legion had entered at the request of the citizens of Jerusalem. As previously mentioned, Lt Colonel Slade was wounded in the fighting at Sheikh Jerrah. He was replaced by Major Desmond Buchanan, also from the Grenadier Guards, who was wounded a few hours later. I remained at the original Regimental Headquarters in the outer suburbs of the city. Surprisingly, ecclesiastical life in Jerusalem continued on its normal path. The next day was Palm Sunday. I wandered down towards St Stephen's Gate in the morning and climbed the steep slope into Jerusalem, where I looked to see whether the Israelis were behaving themselves, but it was not the Israelis but the antics of a donkey which claimed my attention. As I climbed the hill, behind me came the Latin Patriarch in full robes, riding a donkey. I had not realised that this was the route he had chosen to take, presumably because of the heavy fighting that had gone on in the Old City. When the donkey had climbed just under the crest of the hill, she said that she had had enough. All kinds of pious and holy men, accompanying the Patriarch on foot, gathered round behind the donkey and started to push. Now it happened that they had none of the necessary equipment, as they have at Ascot and Epsom, to push recalcitrant animals into the stalls. The donkey accepted the attentions of the pious and holy men, many of whom were tonsured, until her patience finally snapped, and she lashed out with both hind legs, catching one of the holy men in that part of his anatomy which would ensure that he would never again be led into temptation. He was carried off by the others, groaning, and I took the opportunity to run down the hill to the road that led up from Bethany, where I was lucky in finding a 15-hundredweight truck full of soldiers from my Regiment. I made them de-bus and pile their arms. We then doubled up the hill, and I was able to show the Bedouin soldiers what the position was. They understood in a flash. Donkeys are part of their lives. They lined up on each side of the donkey and carried her, Patriarch still up, over the crest of the hill, where she made good progress down to the Church of the Holy Sepulchre. If I had been quick on the

Members of the Desert Reconnaissance Squadron.

uptake, like a Member of Parliament, I would have asked His Beatitude for a plenary indulgence, but I was not quick enough and lost the opportunity. This was a prime example of Islamic and Christian co-operation.

Bob Slade recovered from his minor wounds, and was able to retake command of the 2nd Regiment in due course. Desmond Buchanan, who was a contract officer, retired from the fray at that time.

When the mandate ended in 1948, an Egyptian brigade occupied the area of Hebron and Bethlehem in Transjordan. Nakrashi Pasha was then Prime Minister of Egypt. They stopped an ammunition ship bound for Jordan in early May 1948, and they sent a brigade to occupy Hebron and Bethlehem in southern Jordan, but soon withdrew to Egypt, having stopped the payment of money promised to Jordan by the Arab League. I was sent to clear up the mess and to ensure that the last of the Egyptian troops had left. I found the inhabitants of Bethlehem somewhat difficult and quarrelsome, but had not experienced any difficulties with them. We took over after the Egyptians had withdrawn, so in the space of a few days I became like Pontius Pilate, ex officio Governor of Hebron and Bethlehem.

4

Jerusalem and After, 1948

A t the time when the Arab Legion became involved in the battles for the control of Palestine, the Foreign Secretary was Ernest Bevin, who was one of the Labour Party's brightest appointees to an all-important ministry. Ernest Bevin was a steadfast supporter of the Palestinians fighting for their existence against the Israelis in Palestine, before the recognition of Israel by the United Nations, which de facto meant the United States. He came under pressure politically to withdraw all British officers from involvement in anticipated fighting between the Israelis and the Jordanians and Palestinian Arabs. The House of Commons had been anxious to avoid the political difficulties which would have been caused by the involvement of the largely British-officered Arab Legion, which was expected to bear the brunt of the fighting both in the city of Jerusalem and the rest of Palestine.

King Abdullah had come under great pressure from the citizens of Jerusalem to relieve them from attempts by the Israelis to seize all the Old and New cities. When the King decided to enter Jerusalem, the whole conflict was unexpected, tactically, and the Jordanians were much hampered by obstacles in the shape of massive buildings, which were to be rescued from Israeli control. The Arab Legion, as it was then composed, was trained to fight in the desert, not in major towns and cities. British officers were in the lead, and suffered casualties in the early attacks, Colonel Slade among them. At the same time, many volunteers arrived in Palestine to fight against the Israelis. One of these was Major Geoffrey Lockett, who had distinguished himself with the Chindits in Burma. He had replaced Colonel Slade as Commander of the 2nd Regiment after the latter's injury. Geoffrey had won a Bar to his Distinguished Service Order when fighting with the Chindits. He was a very welcome addition to the Jordanian Army, where he further distinguished himself. One of the first things that he had done was to blow up the pumping station which supplied water to the New City from the plain immediately to the west. Its repair and maintenance were important to the New City.

Soon after 3rd Brigade returned from Jerusalem, there were many interested visitors, including Freya Stark, who arrived hot-foot to see how things were going. Freya got on very well with Teal Ashton, because she had a predilection for homosexual men, of whom Teal was one. In addition, we were visited by various Sheikhs of the Shemar tribe from the north of the Hejaz; everyone wanted to know what had happened in Jerusalem. Teal gave a luncheon party for the visitors, particularly from the al Rhashid, the Shemar Sheikhs who were in power at that time. King Abdullah was anxious to visit the 3rd Brigade in the Jordan Valley at Nebi Musa, a place where the Prophet Moses is reckoned to be buried, and not too far from King Abdullah's palace at Shuneh.

The Brigade moved to Nebi Musa, but had only just arrived when a violent storm, with heavy rain, blew all the tents flat, just before the royal inspection. King Abdullah was quite unmoved by this situation. He shrugged his shoulders and said, 'These things happen in the desert at any time.'

The widespread flooding in the Jordan Valley brought in some unexpected wildlife. I well remember shooting at a pair of widgeon flying past. I aimed for the drake, but the duck fell stone dead. That put me in my place. It was a really bad shot.

The Chief Staff Officer of the Division came down to see us, accompanied by two dachshund dogs. Soon after he arrived, a golden eagle flew in and was obviously very interested in having dachshund for dinner. She was joined by her mate, and they pitched in very close to the two dogs. I was very afraid that they were going to try to kill them, but fortunately they funked it and the dachshunds got off unscathed. However, it was a narrow escape, and the officer concerned had not realised the situation. Fortunately, all had been well.

The Government had got into a nervous state over the presence of British officers serving in the Arab Legion, with the responsibility resting with Ernest Bevin, probably the best Foreign Secretary that England had seen for some time. The Divisional Commander, Norman Lash, summoned all British officers serving in the Arab Legion, of which I was one, to collect at the Allenby Bridge over the River Jordan. When we reached the Allenby Bridge, we were told to stand in the middle of it until further notice. It so happened that at that moment the Foreign Secretary, answering a question in the House of Commons, stated that there were no British officers on either bank of the River Jordan. I presumed that the same arrangements had been made at the Sheikh Hussein Bridge higher up the river, so the House of Commons was not misled. I remember this well as I, personally, was bitten by an Anopheles mosquito and developed malaria, which was diagnosed and treated in the Divisional Headquarters Clinic at Ramala.

It was about that time that Aneurin Bevan, an out-and-out socialist of the most intense variety, was flying up the River Jordan, and a rather socialist lady, who I can remember wearing leather boots, remarked apropos of Bevan that he was his own worst enemy. Quick as a flash, Ernest Bevin, who was listening, as I was, exclaimed, 'Not while I am alive, 'e aint.'

5

Lydda and Ramle, 1948

The Israelis had occupied both Lydda and part of Ramle, and as was their usual habit were driving out all the civil population to fend for itself. This caused considerable agitation, in both Jordan and the rest of Arab Palestine. The 5th Garrison Company was withdrawn to join me outside Ramle.

I was extremely upset, as I would have liked to destroy the Israeli colony at Ben Shemen, but that had been refused. While I was still at Ramle, I decided that as a diversion, and without the authority of the Brigade, I would destroy the Israeli colony at Qeezer, which overlooks the main road to Jerusalem, north of Khulda.

I started by destroying their electric generator plant with anti-tank guns, but when we entered their minefields many Palestinian irregulars followed us and regrettably took some casualties, as the mines were above ground with trip wires.

We were also shelled by our own artillery, which was under the command of 4th Regiment, which was not notified of our attack.

At the colony there was a large chicken farm on its north side, and many of the irregulars following us were seen with arms full of white Leghorns. My unauthorised attack caused a great deal of mayhem in Israeli circles, but we were not able to consolidate by annexing territory, and eventually withdrew.

I was also upset that the Arab Legion artillery fired some valuable shells at us, which fortunately failed to explode in the soft valley bottom. We lost an armoured-car commander, who threw a grenade at the Israelis and did not give himself time to duck back into his turret.

On my return to 3rd Brigade Headquarters, I argued with Teal, who accused me of incurring unnecessary casualties. However, that came to nothing and I resumed my activities at Yalu and Latroun, where there were problems with convoys, which were authorised by the United Nations to get up the road to Jerusalem. On one occasion, the Sergeant Major of 2nd Regiment restrained one of his soldiers, who had pulled the pin out of a primed grenade and threatened to throw it, but that was settled without further mishap.

While all this was going on the Israelis raided Qibliya village, north-west of Ramallah. Teal, unfortunately, did not leave his headquarters, which was the wrong thing to do in any case, but he was heavily criticised for this by those who felt that he should have directed the battle, which, in fact, he left to the Commanding Officer of 12th Regiment, who was not particularly active in counter-attacking. Arab Legion Headquarters, under pressure, convened a court of enquiry to discover what had gone wrong. Meanwhile, the Israelis were sending an increased number of convoys to Jerusalem, and we suspected that they were cheating, as many of the supplies were probably of military value.

At about this time, the United Nations became involved in the peacekeeping efforts to relieve Jerusalem. We understood that Count Bernadotte would become the Chief UN mediator, and we were joined by many of his staff, including the Chief of the Swedish General Staff, Count Bonde.

During this period, more control over the convoys to Jerusalem was exercised. Count Bernadotte put up a paper to the United Nations proposing moves to regulate the supply of food to Jerusalem. But his good work was curtailed by his murder.

We all thought that the murder of Count Bernadotte would have had some effect on the Israelis, but no one really understood the power of the Israeli lobby in Washington, so the Count's life counted for nothing. Bernadotte's replacement as mediator was a black American called Dr Ralph Bunche, who sensibly chose to position himself well clear of Palestine with the protection of a good band of blue water. Dr Bunche left a tough US Marine Brigadier General called Riley to occupy the UN Headquarters, the former

Government House in Jerusalem, and he recommended everything that Washington wanted him to. Bunche negotiated one of the frequent truces between the Israelis and the Egyptians which were inevitably broken by one side or the other. As I understood it at the time, that stretch of the Negev Desert which runs south to the Gulf of Aqaba had been allotted to the Arabs in the original UN partition.

The shooting truce went on as before. I well remember when 2nd Regiment, then under Lockett, was told by some Palestinian farmers that the Israelis would not allow them to harvest their crops. I concealed two medium machine guns in a cave which overlooked the area. When the time came to reap, the Israelis attacked and were wiped out by our machine guns. For that I received a reprimand from the UN mediator, but I also had a letter from Glubb Pasha saying, 'Well done.'

At that time, our whole strategy depended on holding the Latroun Salient. Shortly after this, we were visited by Field Marshal Sir John Harding, Chief of the Imperial General Staff, who told me that the court of enquiry had found that Teal was, in part, responsible for the failure to defend Qibliya against the Israeli raid and massacre. He also said that Glubb Pasha had asked for me to attend the Staff College course at Camberley, which was due to start at the beginning of January 1954.

In addition to Lockett, we also had as a new volunteer an ex-Grenadier called Desmond Buchanan. Teal Ashton, now the Brigade Commander, had two deputies, the most

Serving coffee in a Bedouin tent.

important being Lockett, and he was extremely concerned about our lack of manpower, and felt we should avoid getting into too many battles, preserving as many of our soldiers as we could.

At that stage, Lydda was strongly held by a Palestinian garrison, and the Palestinians were keen to branch out over the adjoining plain. The 3rd Brigade moved into a position south of Lydda. The 4th Regiment was attacked by the Israelis in its position near Latroun. The Israelis moved their force for the attack in half-track armoured vehicles. The 4th Regiment battled against them for all of one night, and destroyed a large number of Israelis and the half-track vehicles. During the attack there was movement on the flanks of our position around Yalu village, and Israeli reinforcements arrived by bus. When the attackers disembarked, it quickly became apparent that they had no knowledge of what they were doing. We rounded up many Israelis, some of whom were actually taking cover in a hedge of prickly pears. It materialised that these Israelis came out of a newly arrived immigrant ship further north. They should never have been sent to the battle, and eventually finished up in our prisoner-of-war cages. Whoever authorised the despatch of these wretched civilians to the battlefront must have had no respect for their own people.

Teal gave me a roving commission to report on the progress of the Israeli offensive in the immediate area, following the debacle of the unsuccessful attack on the 4th Regiment. My immediate task was to stop the shelling of our positions from an area adjoining Sarafand Camp. This I succeeded in doing, as I knew the ground through hunting with the Ramle Vale Hounds. I ran the OP (observation post) to earth in a large tower of sandbags adjoining the wire of Sarafand Camp, and shot it out with an armoured-car gun. This relieved the pressure in our own backyard. From there I moved, taking with me an armoured car and a Jeep, to the area of Yehudiya village, where, despite a truce, I found a scout car, which had been captured from the Palestine Police fighting against the local Arabs. This was around the period which Glubb Pasha described as the 'shooting truce'.

One of the difficulties that faced us was that the Palestinians became our immediate allies, and they were totally ill-disciplined. We never knew what they were going to do next.

The most disciplined were those who had sensible mayors directing operations in their own towns. The municipality of Ramle was well organised and competent. In Lydda the leaders of the municipality were divided and often at each other's throats.

The area headquarters of the Palestine Police, which was in a fort to the west of Lydda, was still operational. Further west there was the Israeli colony of Ben Shemen, which had been strategically placed to cover the main road from Tel Aviv to the east. The Palestine Police Commander was very much on the side of the Arabs fighting for Lydda and Ramle. We used the Police Headquarters, including the prison, to house any prisoners that we had been forced to take during the course of our operations. Immediately to the west of the Police District Headquarters there was an Israeli colony straddling a main road, one of many that had been intentionally placed there against the possibility of a final British withdrawal. I had requested authority from Brigade Headquarters to attack this colony, but had been refused permission, as the Brigadier had decided not to get into immediate hostilities with any Israeli colonies in case we further depleted our available manpower by taking too many casualties. All the Israelis who had been taken prisoner in the fighting so far had been incarcerated in the Police Headquarters building. Unfortunately, among the prisoners held there were some very attractive young women who had caught the eyes of many of my soldiers. The following night I was woken by a frantic call from Police Headquarters, where one of my armoured-car commanders had been threatening to shoot the Police Commander unless he was allowed access to the prisoners. This was a serious case of ill-discipline among my soldiers, and I was anxious about the future. As I had no authority to attack Ben Shemen, I decided that the best tactic was to hand over whatever prisoners we held to the colonists. On the following morning, I went in a Jeep and an armoured car, with a white flag, accompanied by a captured bus full of Israeli prisoners to the wire fence at the edge of Ben Shemen. I then handed the prisoners in, many of them suffering from minor injuries. The colony was willing to accept them, so I was able to relieve the Palestine Police Headquarters of the difficulty of holding a large number of prisoners, many of them women, and at the same time put pressure on Ben Shemen to accept a number of extra non-combatants. At that stage I was still in my British Army uniform, and the colonist whom we contacted first was anxious to shoot me, but was dissuaded by the two-pounder gun of the armoured car.

On 8 June, I took a composite company to Ramle, which had been held since the start of the fighting by its own-armed citizens, supported by two bodies of Bedouin irregulars from Jordan.

The two towns of Lydda and Ramle are on the coastal plain not very far from Jaffa and Tel Aviv, and the main road to Jerusalem passes through the middle of Ramle. The Israeli forces were fully engaged in Jerusalem and in attacking the Latroun Salient, in addition to countering the threat from the Iraqi Brigade to the north, and the Egyptian forces, for what they were worth, in the south. It had been a considerable risk for the Israelis to have left Lydda and Ramle alone. The Israelis, backed as they were by the United States, had a much more realistic idea of the ability of the Security Council and the United Nations to influence events than we had, particularly as the Arab Legion was paid for by Her Majesty's Government, which had the power to cut off the funds at any time. This was very inhibiting to our operations, and we were under strict orders to confine ourselves to working within the borders laid down by the United Nations for the partition of Palestine.

On arrival in Ramle, I had decided to occupy a position astride the main road leading into the city from the west. While the men were digging, we were heavily mortared. Fortunately, many of the bombs failed to detonate in the sandy soil. I would not have been much good as James Bond, who would instantaneously have dived for cover on seeing the tail of an unexploded mortar bomb quivering in the sand at his feet. Fortunately, we escaped with only one fatal casualty, but digging was disrupted. I could not see how the Israelis could have been observing us through the thick orange and olive groves that surround that area, but, throwing caution to the wind, I took an armoured car, and driving westwards under a railway bridge, found a track leading straight into the orange groves. We turned up the track and were lucky to strike gold first time, coming across an observation post built on a tower of sandbags. This I demolished and we retreated to our positions, where the men spent the rest of the morning completing their fortifications unembarrassed by further attacks. The rest of that day was spent looking around the area and talking to the commanders of the irregular forces at the two towns, as well as with the local Police Commander, who was still wearing a Palestine Police uniform, at the old Police Headquarters on the Ramle–Lydda road. It struck me that with Ben Shemen just north-east of Lydda, the town would always be highly vulnerable to a flanking attack. We could have taken that colony, and I asked for permission to do so, but I was flatly refused, presumably because of the danger of incurring heavy casualties. Whether Lydda and Ramle could have been held subsequently if we had demolished the colony was doubtful, but we would certainly have made the Israelis' task very much harder.

Having talked to the mayors and leaders in the two towns and the Sheikhs of the various Bedouin irregular forces, I came to the conclusion that something offensive had to be done to maintain their morale. We heard that a truce under UN auspices was to come into effect early on the morning of 11 June. The best target appeared to be a small Israeli colony called Gizzeh, which lay to the south of the Ramle–Latroun road near the village of Al Barriya. I decided to attack the colony in the early afternoon of the following day. For security reasons we used only Bedouin irregulars in addition to our own company. The attack went well, and the colony was duly taken after about two hours' fighting.

Bedouin boy with goat.

Having been refused permission to take Ben Shemen, I deliberately refrained from telling Brigade Headquarters of our intention. An unfortunate result of this was that we came under some intermittent long-range fire from our own artillery in the Latroun area. Fortunately, no damage was done, although we lost two men in the attack. Having taken the colony, we handed it over to the irregulars, who looted it while we withdrew to Ramle.

That evening the commander of the town force at Lydda came to see me to say that he was planning an offensive against Sarafand Camp and as far north as Beit Dajan. He asked me if the armoured cars could support the attack on Sarafand Camp from an area directly south of the Lydda–Ramle road. I demurred somewhat, as there appeared very little time between dawn and six o'clock, when the truce was due to start. Soon after dawn the following morning I was awakened by heavy fire from the north, and realised that the irregulars were going in alone. I took our armoured-car troop into the battle to give them fire support, which was lucky as it enabled their men to withdraw from an extremely difficult position. The problem with the irregulars was that they had little discipline and no military training, although they were extremely brave. They had absolutely no chance of succeeding in breaking through to Sarafand Camp, which was heavily fortified. I suspected that those manning the fortifications were equally inexperienced, but they were in fortified defensive positions, and the irregulars were not. Having extricated the Lydda forces I was told by their commander that his excursion towards Beit Dajan had failed and the Israelis were forcing his men back under pressure. So, taking one armoured car, I drove to the village of Yehudiya, beyond which the road forks, one way leading south-west to Beit Dajan, the other due west to Tel Aviv. Here we stopped to review the situation, only to see an Israeli armoured personnel carrier, with a machine gun mounted in the turret, driving some irregular troops in front of it and firing as it went. This was in clear contravention of the truce, which should have started three hours before, and I had no hesitation in ordering the armoured car to destroy the offending vehicle. This it did, perhaps too effectively, as when it was towed in to a workshop in Lydda it was too badly damaged to be repaired and used by the irregulars.

The following day a telegram arrived from Brigade Headquarters to the effect that my composite force had to hand over to the 5th Garrison Company, which originally provided me with one platoon. On the way back to Latroun I stopped at Brigade Headquarters, only to receive an imperial rocket from the Brigadier, who was livid that we had two men killed and that the settlement that we sacked was, in fact, outside the area originally allocated to the Arabs by the United Nations.

The truce was to last initially for a month, with the expectation that it would continue and that hostilities would not be resumed. The terms stated that there were to be no reinforcements by either side, and no improvement of military positions. The Israelis were banned from re-supplying Jerusalem with anything more than a subsistence level of food and medical supplies during the period. A UN embargo on the supply of arms, ammunition and money to any Middle Eastern country bordering on Palestine was earlier announced. Food convoys to Jerusalem were under the control of the Armistice Commission headed by Count Bernadotte, which was overseeing the observance of the truce. These convoys were driven up the old Jerusalem road under the noses of our troops, who were somewhat bitter to see the enemy being able to re-supply in this way. It soon became apparent that the Israelis had little or no intention of keeping to the terms of the truce. Nor would our soldiers have done so if we had not kept them very firmly under control. When the first convoy drove past, accompanied by a member of the Armistice Commission and under a white flag, one of our soldiers, an Ageidi from Southern Syria, decided that he personally would stop the nonsense, and rushed down towards the road with a Mills grenade in each hand, from which he had extracted the pins with his teeth. He was hotly pursued by the Regimental Sergeant Major and me, and we spent some three-quarters of an hour arguing with the wretched man within a few yards of the road before he was persuaded to change his mind. Even then, it was with some difficulty that we neutralised his grenades. Since then I always have the deepest sympathy with policemen and others who have to deal with armed maniacs threatening hostages or their families.

The Israelis started building fortifications, in defiance of the Armistice terms, on a ridge facing Latroun at a distance of some three thousand yards. I spent one afternoon sitting on the seat of an Oerlikon anti-aircraft gun, shooting at the diggers with 20mm shells. This put a prompt end to their activities, but the Israelis answered by firing two or three Spandaus at me. The bullets hummed by like angry hornets, but there was no accuracy at that extreme range and I ended my afternoon's entertainment unscathed. We came to know the senior members of the Armistice Commission quite well. Count Bernadotte, himself, who was very closely related to the King of Sweden, was an unpretentious and charming aristocrat determined to try to make the truce stick. His Chief of Staff, Count Bonde, a colonel, was a very active and bright spark who was to become some years later Chief of the Swedish General Staff. The officer who dealt directly with us on a daily basis was a Colonel Bernstein, with whom we established a reasonably close rapport.

As the end of the truce period approached, there was a meeting of the Arab League in Cairo, at which we expected agreement would be reached for hostilities to cease on a permanent basis. We had not bargained for the stupidity and perfidy of Nakrashi Pasha, the Egyptian Premier, or his stooge Abdul Rahman Assam Pasha, nominated as secretary of the Arab League, who, because they were afraid of Egyptian public opinion, insisted upon proceeding with the war, against the advice of all the military leaders. Matters were not helped by the Lebanese Premier Riad al Solh, who had a loud mouth and no involvement in the war, and kept shouting that Palestine should be defended to the last drop of Arab blood. So it was determined that hostilities would be resumed, and we all knew that it would be to our cost.

One of the events that happened during the period of the truce was that a regular colonel from the American Army, who was commanding a brigade in the area facing Latroun, was killed by one of his own sentries. This caused considerable consternation among the Israelis, but in fact the erring sentry did his country a great service as the Colonel was strategically and tactically incompetent, and we had been pleased to have him on the other side. How Truman and Dean Rusk had the temerity to put pressure on Ernest Bevin to withdraw British serving officers of the Arab Legion to the East Bank of the Jordan while a serving US Army officer commanded troops in Israel I never did discover, but politicians have always been corrupt in their own interests. Truman was certainly no exception.

Hostilities resumed on 9 July 1948, and the Israeli pincer movement to capture Lydda and Ramle which I had tried to pre-empt just before the truce started swung into action. The Israeli forces quickly overran the two towns, despite a rear-guard action by the 5th Garrison Company and the intervention of a squadron of armoured cars from the 1st Regiment. Even before we heard officially that the two towns had fallen we saw long lines of refugees, mainly women and children, moving across the plain towards our positions. On 11 July I was asked to take our squadron of armoured cars on a long-distance patrol to see where the Israelis had reached. We drove up a track to the village of

Jimzu, about eight kilometres due east of Ramle, where the commander of my leading armoured car saw some Israeli movement. Coming round the village cross-country we ran into a group of Israelis quenching their thirst at the village well. We were able to annihilate these, but heavy fire from the village proved that a considerable number of troops occupied it. We then returned to Latroun, and I was able to warn the Brigade Commander to expect the enemy to arrive and attempt to cut the main road between Latroun and Beit Sira within a matter of days. This duly happened, and on the fifteenth we suspected enemy movement near the village of Salbit, to which I took a fighting patrol just after midnight. The Israelis were in occupation, but we surprised them and were able to inflict casualties. Unfortunately, one of my sergeants, Mehsin from the Beni Sakhr tribe, the main Bedouin tribe in Jordan, was killed by a grenade which exploded between us. The shrapnel wounded me in the head, but we were able to kill the Israeli who had thrown it. That night the Israelis occupied the village of Al Burj, which overlooks the vital Beit Sira junction on the Latroun–Ramallah road. The Brigade Commander decided to stop the Israelis in their tracks here. The 2nd Regiment was ordered to carry out a set-piece attack on Al Burj the following afternoon. The attack was successful, and the Israelis were beaten back with heavy casualties. Unfortunately, I missed that battle, having been *hors de combat* with my head wound, but all our troops distinguished themselves. Hamdan al Blewi, the armoured-car Squadron

Commander, from the Billi tribe in the northern Hejaz, was seriously wounded in the legs when he drove over a mine. When I returned to the United Kingdom, my mother, who had been in charge of a hospital in Gretna Green during the First World War, insisted that I have the shrapnel removed, as she was worried that it might travel to the area of my brain.

6

Aqaba and the
Wadi Araba, 1948

Soon after we returned to Amman, I was asked to see
Glubb Pasha in his office, where he told me that I
was to command a mixed force to go to the Wadi
Araba to prevent any Israeli advance into this area from the
north. I could not understand why we were doing this, but
subsequently discovered that the whole of the northern part
of the Araba had been allocated to Jordan in the original
settlement over Palestine. I went to see the Pasha's Chief of
Staff, Lt Colonel Charles Coaker, RA, who told me what
I was to do and then said, 'The Pasha says, you are on no
account to risk a defeat,' which was a very unlikely order to
an officer who was just about to take control of a large slice
of southern Jordan.

An Auster aircraft was made available to fly me down the
length of the Wadi to give me a general idea of the ground,
which stretches from the south coast of the Dead Sea to the

A baggage camel near the Dead Sea.

Gulf of Aqaba. The pilot flew brilliantly, keeping well below the steep sides of the Wadi to enable me to pick out any important features in the bed, which varies between three and seven miles wide.

By this time the Israelis had comprehensively defeated the Egyptian Army, despite posturing from the UN peacekeepers ensconced in Rhodes after the murder of Count Bernadotte.

Part of my force, a scratch company commanded by Lieutenant Suliman Jarad, was already assembled at Aqaba. With a call to my driver, Ibrahim Ali and my soldier servant Abdullah bin Abdul Kerim, with a light truck and my Alsatian dog, Rex, they joined me the next day in Amman. Thence the long drive to Maan and Aqaba down the desert road. Eight hours of dust and discomfort before reaching Maan and subsequently Aqaba, where the scratch company was assembled, as was a modicum of transport, two troops of armoured cars and some support weapons, which were provided from the 3rd Regiment. Maan was so full of bed bugs, which lived in the mud walls of the town, including the railway and police stations, that I asked Abdullah to make up my bed some forty paces away from any building, which I thought was too far for a bed bug to walk in the night, and so I slept with immunity from that particular plague. This continued all the time I was in Aqaba and subsequently the Wadi Araba.

Our first task was to negotiate with local contractors for the supply of food, on a daily basis, and fuel for our vehicles. I chose my provisional position almost due west of the Desert Police post of Gharandal, on the Jordanian side of the Wadi Araba. The next task was to move the troops, for which the existing transport was totally inadequate. A shipping firm called Abuzaid and Nezal was established at Aqaba. It used to unload the cargos of ships arriving at the port, and despatch them by the desert road to the railhead at Ras al Negb (the top of the pass). From there the goods were moved by rail to Amman. I arranged with Abuzaid and Nezal to borrow a large lorry called a Mac from them, in which I accommodated all the force that I had been given. We had no one to drive it, except for me, so I drove all the troops up the Wadi Araba, north of Aqaba, until we reached a salt marsh called Hadh Haudha, which has the same name as the great salt marsh in the desert adjoining Jordan and Saudi Araba. I found the

Mac rather easy to drive, and was fortunate to be able to reach the area in which I wanted to establish my position north of Aqaba. I moved my force, with the only officer given to me, one Suliman Jarad from the Bedul, a tribe that occupied Wadi Musa. I rested the right flank of my force north of Hadh Haudha at the existing fort occupied by the Desert Police at Gharandal on the east side of the Araba. The first night after we had arrived all hell was let loose by my soldiers, who were firing wildly. I could not understand from whence the enemy came. It turned out to have been an unfortunate cheetah, which had wandered into our lines in the night and was duly slaughtered, and its skin sold in Aqaba.

Lieutenant Ghazi al Harbi, a distinguished officer of the 3rd Regiment, arrived from Amman. He had been the Commander of the company that had reached the Monastery of Notre Dame in Jerusalem during the recent fighting, but had been ordered to withdraw from such a precarious position after reaching stalemate. Ghazi al Harbi was determined that the withdrawal was some sort of a plot by his British Commanding Officer, and that he should have stayed where he was in a clearly vulnerable position after reaching stalemate. He had made such a nuisance of himself that the Pasha sacked him. Subsequently he managed to transfer to the Saudi Arabian Army, and was only given to me, I suspected, as the Wadi Araba was a place in which he could do no harm. I liked Ghazi al Harbi, despite his obstinacy, and visited him after he moved to Jeddah, where he was then a Major in the Saudi Arabian Royal Guard. I next met him in Riyadh, where he had risen to the rank of Colonel and was Deputy Commander of the Royal Guard there. He died many years later at the military hospital in Riyadh.

While the soldiers were preparing our defensive position, I was able to reconnoitre the ground to the north. It was then that we were joined by the squadron of armoured cars, infantry company and support weapons from the 3rd Regiment. This enabled us to position a screen of armoured cars on another ridge some thirty miles to the north. We were also joined by a strong band of Howeitat irregulars nominally under the command of Lieutenant Sager Abtan, a Howeitat Sheikh who had been a Lieutenant in the Desert Police. Among the irregulars were a number of Howeitat Sheikhs who had already distinguished themselves in early battles at Bab al Wad and Latroun. These had included Jadour al Audat, Rafafan bin Ali and Goftan bin Jazi, who were positioned further north-east on a reddish ridge of rocks called Hamra Ifdan.

Having established ourselves north of Aqaba we proceeded to reconnoitre as far as north as we could. I was a bit concerned at the time over where we stood with the Egyptian Army. Egyptian aircraft were quite active over our positions, but apart from the odd bomb they represented no threat.

North of Gharandal we were joined by a force of Howeitat Bedouins who joined us on a promise made by Glubb Pasha. They had stayed with us for the rest of our time in the Wadi. It was about this time that I borrowed two riding camels from the Desert Police and rode them to the north along an ancient track that is covered in the hieroglyphics of Bedouin tribesmen, I would think, from the days of the Nabateans. That subsidiary valley runs up to Shobek in the Shera Mountains, which at that time of the winter are intermittently covered with snow and ice. It was quite difficult in these circumstances to adjust from the heat of the Wadi Araba to the cold temperatures of the Shera Mountains. Going up the Wadi I found a migrating teal sitting on the edge, and having had nothing for dinner I shot him with a .303 rifle from the back of my camel. The bullet must have just grazed his head and killed him instantly. He did not make a very good luncheon, but we ate him all the same. Once I had shot the teal, the camel on which I was riding suddenly sprang up, all four legs in the air, as it had taken her all that time to hear my shot.

The Assistant Commander of the Jordan Police at Maan was the son of Abdul Quader Pasha al Jundi, a tough old Turkish warrior who had been second-in-command of the Arab Legion to Glubb Pasha. To the north of our position, near Gharandal, we were joined by some Howeitat irregulars, under their various sheikhs who were all from the main sub-Tribe of the Howeitat and who stayed with us for the rest of our time in the Araba. They were very useful to us in gaining intelligence when the Israelis decided to move against us from south of the Hebron district. At that time, I was told that some Egyptian Bedouins from the Sinai Desert were spying on us. We rounded them up and sent them to the local Bedouin Magistrate at Quweira. I never discovered what happened to them, but we certainly never heard of them again.

7

Operations in the
Wadi Araba, 1948

We still had no word of Israeli movement in the Negev. The problem was that there was no dissemination of information, as it is called in Staff College. We were left entirely in the dark on what was happening to the north of us, but one rather odd event was that a light aircraft landed just north of where we were encamped and subsequently took off again before we had time to shoot at it. At about the same time a Royal Navy frigate arrived at Aqaba. I visited the ship and made myself known to the Commander. I was a little uneasy about what the Egyptians were up to, but no further danger appeared from the Sinai Desert. The Howeitat Bedouins reported movement of Israeli forces to the west and south-west of Ain Hasb.

There was a great deal of Israeli movement to the north of us, so I positioned observers and some armoured cars on the first major hills south of Ain Hasb. I deployed my armoured cars as a screen to the north, from where I expected the Israelis would move south. We did not hear any Israeli movement until later on, when a reconnaissance patrol arrived not very far from Gharandal Police Fort and came across the light aircraft on a mud flat in the middle of the Wadi, and were unable to stop it escaping. I was informed that a force of Israelis had reached Ain Hasb, in the Wadi Araba just south of the Dead Sea. I took my Jeep and an escort with me, and we found where an Israeli patrol had spent the night and failed to cover its tracks, including where it had had a meal the evening before.

The Israeli patrols became more active and more daring. I decided to use a line of high ground to the north of the Wadi Araba as my first line of defence. Unfortunately, my flanks were completely exposed. In order to cover the east flank, I decided to lay a minefield in the main bed of the Wadi. I was given a large number of anti-tank mines, which had been manufactured in the Arab Legion depot outside Amman. The mines had crush fuses, which were inefficient and dangerous, but I took the risk of using them, mistakenly as it turned out. Our Engineer Corporal was given the task of sowing the mines in the Wadi bottom, just south and east of our position. He just reported to me that the mines were laid when there was a huge explosion; it transpired that he had trodden on one of his own mines which, although it was meant to be an anti-tank mine, exploded far too easily. The explosion blew the legs off the Engineer Corporal, and two of my officers were badly injured. The Engineer Corporal died almost immediately of shock. I asked the Commander of the frigate to take the two officers to Fayid in the Canal Zone. One of them was badly affected by tetanus, but they both emerged safely in the end. I was most grateful to the Royal Navy for saving the lives of those two officers. As far as I know, they are still with us now. We withdrew from the Araba without further mishap, only to discover that Norman Lash, who commanded the Arab Legion Division, had been replaced by a new British Major General.

After that, events on our northern border came quickly. The Israelis sent a party down our right flank. We had news of these from our Bedouin friends. They skirted our positions and went deep into our territory. A party of Israelis crossed the Egyptian border, where they bivouacked for the night and did not hide their refuse which made me think that we could expect more of them in the near future. I was joined by an ex member of the Desert Police, called Abu Sheikh, from the Jebli tribe from an area north of H5, a pumping station on the old pipeline from Iraq to Jordan. I sent him down to defend a disused fortified encampment in the mountains east of Aqaba. It may have been the same encampment used by the Turks against Lawrence in the First World War. We constructed our positions so that we could cover the main track with our armoured cars, and rested our right flank on the salt marsh and behind that the Desert Police station at Gharandal. I contacted Arab Legion Headquarters and asked what I was to do about the various threats. I collected our wheeled transport and sent it back to Aqaba so that we had no soft underbelly in case of a full-scale Israeli attack. I asked Headquarters, whether I should withdraw or fight it out as we were, but I never had a constructive answer. In view of the instructions given when we first went down, I decided to withdraw, as I did not want to waste my soldiers' lives unnecessarily. The withdrawal went smoothly, and we left in one night.

8

Fauzi al Mulki's War, 1949

On reaching Maan, I found that a great deal had passed in my absence unreported to me by Arab Legion Headquarters. I discovered that the engineers were digging a road down the side of the Wadi Araba in order to reinforce the Desert Police station at Gharandal. The Israelis had realigned the track at the bottom of the Araba, and the Minister of Defence, Fauzi al Mulki, a veterinary surgeon from Jerusalem, ordered that the realignment should be changed, as the new track entered Jordanian territory for a short distance.

No sooner had I arrived at Maan than I was ordered back to the Wadi Araba with instructions to block the diversion and re-route the Israelis down the original track. In order to achieve the Minister's aims, I was given a squadron of armoured cars from 1st Regiment and a platoon of engineers. By now, winter was upon us and the Shera Mountains, west of Maan, were covered with snow and ice, which was restricting movement of troops and vehicles. I outlined my plan, which was to use wire to close the diversion and re-route the Israelis by the original track.

With my squadron and the engineers came a troop of artillery with towed twenty-five pounder guns. Having discussed with all the officers involved how we were to proceed, and in view of the new road to Gharandal, I decided that I should take the entire force of men and equipment there as quickly as possible. We set off with high hopes of success. It turned out that a new road had been dug by the Arab Legion engineers from Maan to Gharandal. The road was uncomfortably steep, and it was only with great difficulty that our force was able to negotiate the many steep corners which the new road presented to us. I moved the force slowly and carefully, but we lost an armoured car and some of the support vehicles, which failed to turn the corners. Much to my surprise the bulk of my force arrived intact in the Wadi Gharandal, where it dispersed in the bed of the Wadi. However, I was shocked to see my force establishing itself in the Wadi bed, which was always in danger of flooding, particularly in the winter months. That was a timely move, as the Wadi came down that night and the beds of all the force would have been soaked and possibly we would have lost some vehicles.

The plan was to erect the wire barriers and notices as early as we could. Our artillery support remained on top and did not venture down the side of the Wadi, but had enough range to support the force if necessary. The following night we erected our wire barricades and notices, telling the Israelis that we considered that area of the diversion to be part of Jordan. The Israelis did not take kindly to this, and a running battle ensued, as they ignored the instruction that the road was closed. It was not long before shooting started in earnest. I never discovered what they had in mind in reopening the diversion, but there was a long battle between our armoured cars and the enemy, who probably had enough armour piercing weapons to resist us. And resist us they did! Unfortunately, we lost an armoured car, which must have been hit by an armour-piercing weapon of some sort. The Israeli projectile killed the driver and set the vehicle on fire. Not wanting it to fall into Israeli hands, I went myself, in my Jeep, and having opened one of the driver's doors I was able to steer the vehicle by holding the steering wheel, the driver being dead in the seat, which was somewhat of an obstacle. We managed to get one of our armoured personnel carriers, which consisted of an armoured car with a turret removed, and took the damaged vehicle in tow. I had an interesting twenty minutes sitting on the mudguard of the armoured car while the Israelis shot at us with everything they had. They fortunately missed us, and I survived to tell the tale. When I pulled the damaged vehicle back into our lines I was able to release it, as by then it was safe from any Israeli attempts to tow it.

It turned out that the dead driver came from Wadi Musa (Petra village). On my way back to the police station at Gharandal, I was lucky enough to see a golden eagle in action:

there is a little mud flat not too far from the police post, and on that was a flock of McQueen's (Habara) bustards. As I came up, all the birds froze, and I thought I must have made some stupid noise. Not at all, because out of the stratosphere came a noise like an express train and a golden eagle, swooping at very high speed, landed on one unfortunate bustard, killing it instantly. I went to see the eagle's prey, and where its talons had entered the unfortunate bird on each side.

I discovered some time later that in the exchange of fire, a senior Israeli officer had been killed. I suppose that was a fit retaliation, and we completed our withdrawal. Subsequently, the Israelis blew up the Desert Police Fort.

It was a great privilege to meet the Troop Commander of the artillery, Major Max Graham, and he became a lifelong friend. Max noticed that all the chukar partridges had taken refuge from the cold and snow in the rocks immediately below the crest of the Araba. These had whetted Max's appetite for a partridge shoot, which I told him I would reconnoitre in due course. The nature of the ground and the relative scarcity of partridges there made it difficult to organise a shoot, but I found a more suitable place in the area, relatively near Maan, called Bir al Debaghat, which is in the Hishi, a bushy area from which the Turks, before the First World War, extracted wood to fuel the engines of the trains of the Hejaz railway.

In the aftermath of the drama it emerged that Fauzi al Mulki had not told King Abdullah of the operation, and was promptly given the sack.

9

The Departure of Norman Lash
from the Division, 1949

When driving back from Aqaba I met my friend again, and he told me that Norman Lash had been replaced as Divisional Commander. This was bad news for me, as Norman Lash was Glubb Pasha's main British assistant, knew a great deal about the Bedouins, and had long experience in the desert.

Once Norman Lash left, the War Office made many changes in both the structure of the Arab Legion Division and its commanders. The new Commander was Major General Sam Cook, from the Lincolnshire Regiment, who had distinguished himself as an administrator in the Far East and seems to have been regarded as a safe pair of hands to take charge of the Arab Legion Division at that point. There were several indications that Arabists were out of favour because of the new regime. The Brigadiers who were appointed at the same time as General Cook made few bones about their dislike of the original structure of the Division. One of the existing Brigade Commanders was Ski Galetly, whose Brigade was at Mafraq. I was put in Command of the Desert Reconnaissance Squadron, which was formed in response to a plan I put up to Glubb Pasha before I was sent to the Wadi Araba. General Cook, now the Divisional Commander, used to gather the Brigade and Battalion Commanders to Divisional Headquarters for regular discussions and briefings. At one of the first of these, held at Khaw, criticisms were made of the Bedouin who form the backbone of the Division. I was told that in the opinion of many of the newly joined officers, the Bedouins were spoilt, and would be unable to survive for long in the desert, so I undertook to arrange a journey, to be undertaken by many Bedouin units on foot. The plan was to march for some hundred kilometres to the desert fort at Bayer. I set off with the bulk of my Squadron. We travelled two nights and a day in the heat of the Arabian Desert to reach our objective. When we reached Bayer, there were a number of black Bedouin tents pitched on the hill below the Police Fort. I was absolutely exhausted, and delighted when Abdullah bin Abdul Kerim, my soldier servant, pitched my tent below the Police Fort, but I was not to rest for long. Just after dawn, there was a commotion in the black Bedouin tents. A rather irate old Sheikh came to see me, to complain that one of my soldiers had copulated with a young woman of the Tuwayah, a sub-tribe of the Howeitat. It turned out that the offender was an Anezeh from the Dahamsha. The problem here was that many of the Bedouins from the great tribes regarded the Howeitat as somewhat below the salt, and their women as fair game. This, in my opinion, was a lot of nonsense, as the two great divisions of the Howeitat were well-known warriors who had distinguished themselves in past feuds. It is unfortunately a racist myth among the Bedouins. I do not know how the problem was solved, or how the Howeitat were squared. It seems remarkable to me that one of my so-called spoilt, weak Bedouins should have had enough energy to have done the deed in the first place: but it was of great use to me in squashing all talk about spoilt Bedouins.

The powers that be seemed to have decided that the hierarchy within the Division, should be put back on more British lines, and that there should be fewer Arabists in the command structure. Before I left the Wadi Araba, I put a proposal to Glubb Pasha that a unit should be formed on the lines of the Long Range Desert Group in North Africa. The threats, as perceived in military planning, were a Soviet occupation of Iran and Iraq, and led to a need to defend an eastern flank. The planners feared, at that stage, Soviet penetration into Europe through the Mediterranean.

10

Back to the 2nd Regiment and the Shooting Truce, 1949

On my return, I discovered that plans were afoot for me to join the Company Commander's course at Warminster at some future time. I joined the Company Commander's course in the winter of 1949, and was delighted to find a number of my Grenadier friends on the same course, notably Alan Breitmeyer and Sandy Gray.

I found the course more tedious than valuable. While I was in the middle of it, a letter arrived from the authorities in London giving me permission to wear the Jordanian Gallantry Medal, which presumably was granted for my driving the wrecked armoured car back to our lines. As it was already a wreck, I do not know what benefit I gave by driving it back, except that I had caused a very large weight of Israeli ammunition to be expended. The only thing I remember of the course was a highly dangerous shoot arranged in the Warminster area with the idea of reducing the local rabbit population, which is considerable. The only advantage the course gave to me was as preparation for the Staff College, to which there was no inkling that I was to be sent later.

It was the Arab Legion's plan to keep a strong presence in the Latroun Salient. When I returned from the south, Teal Ashton had moved his Brigade Headquarters to the area of Yalu. The 4th Regiment was in Latroun itself, while the 2nd Regiment occupied the hills at Yalu. The 2nd Regiment was under the temporary command of Major Geoffrey Lockett, while the 4th Regiment was commanded by Colonel Habis al Majali.

A few days after our arrival there were two developments. A number of Israelis had entered our position, coming up in buses, as far as Bab al Wad. I thought that it was a sort of attack, but, as mentioned earlier, we quickly rounded up these most unmilitary Israelis, some of whom had only been in Palestine for a few days. I can well remember some of them trying to take shelter in a hedge of prickly pears. We took them all, and eventually sent them back to a prisoner-of-war camp. I had shot at one of the buses with a PIAT mortar. When it was revealed that the occupants were not military, I was delighted that the mortar round had failed to explode.

Simultaneously, the Palestine Police station at Latroun was attacked by Israelis who also attacked 4th Regiment positions overlooking Latroun. These attacks failed through bad timing and bad assessments of the odds, and the 4th Regiment suffered relatively lightly. The Israelis who attacked the Palestine Police station at Latroun with armoured personnel carriers, suffered heavy casualties, as the 4th Regiment defenders threw grenades into the open armoured personnel carriers and forced them to retire. Colonel Habis al Majali was fêted as a hero, and went on, eventually, to become Chief of the Jordanian Armed Forces. The apparent decision of the Israelis to send new refugees into the fighting was, in my opinion, deplorable, and a disgrace to the Israeli Armed Forces.

The battle for Latroun having, at that stage, been won, 3rd Brigade Headquarters was withdrawn from Yalu to the Beit Sira road junction. I was summoned by the Brigade Commander, and was asked to take to Ramle a force of one company and two troops of armoured cars, including a platoon from 4th Regiment, to occupy the town and the area the other side of Police District Headquarters. I was instructed that a truce was to take place almost immediately in the Ramle/Lydda area.

We set off down the road that runs through Qibliya, and at about luncheon time we arrived in Ramle, where I talked to the Mayor, who was organising the defence of his town. At the same time our troops were mortared from somewhere in the region of Sarafand Camp, and one soldier from 4th Regiment was killed. The platoon commander, a young cadet, was extremely upset. I promised him, personally, to deal with the mortar. I knew that piece of the country well, having hunted over it with the Ramle Vale Hunt when I was with the Supernumerary Police. I took my Jeep and an

The author and General Habis al Majali.

armoured car, and drove to a track that I knew on the outside of Sarafand Camp. Sure enough, when I reached the area, I found a large tower of sandbags from which an observation post at the edge of the Camp could overlook the area. I destroyed it with shells from the armoured car, and we were never troubled again from there.

The truce was scheduled to take place just before midday. I took an armoured car and my Jeep to a village called Yehudiya on the main road from Jaffa to Wilhelmina, as I had heard shooting from that area. As I arrived, an ex-Palestine Police armoured car, now in possession of the Israelis, came down the road travelling east from Beit Dajan, firing a machine gun out of the turret. One armour-piercing shell from our armoured car stopped it. Unfortunately, the shell entered the engine, and we were not able to resuscitate it for use by the Palestinian irregulars.

I asked Brigade Headquarters if I was allowed to attack and sack the Israeli settlement at Ben Shemen, but was refused. What I was not told by either Arab Legion Headquarters or 3rd Brigade was that it had been agreed that we should leave Lydda and Ramle undefended. This was a major factor affecting our operations in the area, and we really should have been told. It was, I am afraid, the fault of Arab Legion Headquarters and my own Brigade. I concentrated my force in the area of the Beit Sira road junction, where we awaited events.

11

Staff College and Marriage, 1954–56

In 1954 I was told that I was to join C Division, which was based at Minley Manor. This was very satisfactory for me. The Commander of C Division was Tubby Butler, subsequently General Sir Mervyn Butler, a well-known figure from the Parachute Regiment. I discovered that on the course with me would be many Grenadier friends, some of whom I had last met on the Company Commanders' course, a few weeks before.

I enjoyed myself at the Staff College, mainly because I could relax and absorb the lectures and exercises. The course at Minley Manor was enlivened by the antics of Tubby Butler, who often used to sleep on the grand piano, particularly if there had just been a dinner party. I look back on my time at Minley as a happy period.

Meanwhile there had been a court of enquiry over the lack of action by Teal Ashton when the Israelis invaded our territory and destroyed various houses in Qibliya and returned to their borders without having been engaged by any of the units of the 3rd Arab Legion Brigade. The court of enquiry had found that the Brigade Commander had been negligent. In fact, he was probably right in taking no immediate action, but he should have been on the spot, and appeared to have handled the Brigade in a more belligerent way. If I had been the Brigade Commander, I would certainly have gone to the scene and been more personally active in defending Qibliya village against the Israelis.

At the end of the Staff College course I was joined by Colonel Ian Robertson, who was forming an Arab Legion Staff College to enable the Jordanians to train their officers in their own country.

Ian had been recommended as an instructor at Camberley, and following his course there we took our curriculum and methodology from him. The first course was a success, and subsequent courses took students from other Arab armies.

In December of that year there was a ball at Minley Manor, for those who were studying in C Division at the Staff College. I was asked to take someone with me. I had just taken a week's leave from the Staff College and returned from Le Touquet, and went to stay with my mother in Gloucestershire. I found that she had a house party for a debuntante's dance to which my two younger brothers had been asked. I asked Pamela Kaye, one of the girls staying, and this led to my asking her out to dinner every night the following week.

I then returned to Jordan, but flew back to London in July 1955, and Pamela and I became engaged. I was keen to know whether Pamela would be happy to settle in Jordan, so she came out for a month in October and stayed with the Robertsons, and we went to many places before she flew back to London in the care of Buster Luard. Her mother was waiting for her. In those days the flights to and from

The author with his wife-to-be, at Azraq.

Amman took twelve hours each way. At this time Pamela's great aunt, the Dowager Countess Jellicoe, asked her to go with her on a world tour, which forced Pamela to tell her mother that she could not go on the tour because we were planning to marry in April the following year. Therefore I had to ask her permission to marry her daughter on my return to England on Christmas leave. Also, Pamela very much wanted her old nanny to approve of me. We decided to meet Nanny in the banking hall in Harrods, and we took her out to lunch. Fortunately, Nanny did approve of me, and we were *en rapport*. Subsequently, she was a regular visitor to our house in London.

We were busy making arrangements to live in Zirqa Camp, and Pamela began to send out all our wedding presents, which were subsequently lost, except our bed and bedding, which was not ready. This occurred just as I was about to be promoted Lt Colonel. The Chief of the Imperial General Staff, Sir Gerald Templer, was in Jordan on his way to Iraq to sign a treaty, but his visit was cut short by an attempt by a dissident Jordanian Colonel, Ali Abu Nuwar, to bring down King Hussein's Government and take over the country. The attempt was unsuccessful, as the tribesmen who formed the bulk of the Jordanian Army refused to take part, and eventually succeeded in ousting Ali Abu Nuwar and his revolutionaries. King Hussein emerged stronger than ever. Most of the British officers had left by that time, but I was fortunate enough to be asked to return with my bride.

One of Ali Abu Nuwar's first moves had been to tell Colonel R.K. Melville, the Liaison Officer in London, that my contract with the Jordanian Army was cancelled, and he asked for the return of my army watch, so at that time we had nowhere to live when we returned from our honeymoon. The reason for his wanting to get rid of me was that he was frightened of me because I was so close to the Bedouins.

Templer agreed that I should accompany his party flying back to the United Kingdom, and I telegraphed Pamela in London where she was staying. I had not arrived on the scheduled flight. It was only a week before our wedding, and we had rather a tense time sending messages to and from London as to what the situation was and whether I was going to return in time to be married. All went well, and I was met by one of Sir Gerald's Rolls Royces at London Airport. Tin, my spaniel, and Glubb Pasha's cat flew back with me in the hold of the same aircraft. We were married at the Brompton Oratory on 5 April 1956. Being married on 5 April in those days gave the advantage of tax being remitted over the whole of the preceding year. My housemaster at Ampleforth kindly agreed to marry us in a Jesuit church. One of the obligations placed on me was to arrange for the banns to be read by a Catholic bishop, in due course. This caused some embarrassment later, as the only Catholic bishop I knew was the Latin Patriarch of Jerusalem. I telephoned him and asked for his advice. He referred me to his secretary, who had obviously never heard of banns being read, and jumped to the conclusion that I wanted to marry a Muslim. When he discovered that we were already married, he accused me of wasting the time of His Beatitude the Latin Patriarch. When I ironed out the misunderstanding, he arranged for the banns to be read by the Vicar General in Amman. We spent our honeymoon in France, most of it just outside St Tropez, driving over to Monte Carlo for the wedding of Prince Rainier to Grace Kelly. On our return to London we found a small flat in Eaton Place, into which we moved. We sold our Vauxhall, which we had imported duty free, to an officer who had been posted to Germany, so that no duty had to be paid. We bought an Isetta (a three-wheeled 'bubble car'), because of the shortage of petrol, and we managed to drive to Scotland to shoot with our suitcase on the back and the guns inside. By that point, I had contracted glandular fever and was very ill, taking three months to recover.

After I had fully recovered, I found myself thinking about what I was going to do next. I decided that I would like to apply to re-join the Grenadier Guards. As a first move, I wrote to the Regimental Lt Colonel, Sir Thomas Butler, Baronet, to ask if there was any way I could do so. He was extremely obliging, and a great help to me, so I went through the metamorphosis from the Arab Legion to the Grenadier Guards without too much difficulty. Appointments on the Staff were available to me.

12

Cyprus, 1956

No sooner had we settled in London on my return from the Middle East than a new crisis emerged in Cyprus, where Field Marshall Sir John Harding, now Lord Harding of Penshurst, was Governor.

Immediately after I was reinstated in the Grenadier Guards, the 3rd Battalion was ordered to Cyprus in a peacekeeping role to combat the EOKA terrorists, who were up in arms against the colony and were murdering at least two members of the security forces every week. The situation deteriorated due to the activities of the fiery cleric Archbishop Makarios, who encouraged the Greek Cypriots to rise up against the British colonial Government. We had 24 hours' notice to move.

Pamela had no difficulty in letting go of the Isetta to the then Countess Jellicoe, wife of Earl Jellicoe, because these were much in demand, and she sold the flat to her cousin by marriage, Gerty Wissa.

Michael Colvin was at that time serving in the Grenadier Guards with me, and he too was posted to Cyprus. The 3rd Battalion was flown to Cyprus by Air Trooping, and we went in the first instance to a camp near the Ledra Palace Hotel outside Nicosia. Wives were not allowed to accompany their husbands, but Pamela and her cousin, Nichola Colvin, who was pregnant, ignored that order. Both Pamela and her cousin were extremely upset at having been posted to Cyprus, and as revenge threw their husbands' shoes out of the window of the Ledra Palace, where we were staying in Nicosia for our first married Christmas. Fortunately, the shoes landed on a lean-to addition to the hotel and were easily recovered.

The author's house (white house in the middle) in Kyrenia.

After Christmas we went over to Kyrenia and called in at the Dome Hotel, where we found Costos the head waiter. We asked him if he knew of anywhere we could rent, and he told us that he had a converted carob store in the middle of the harbour which he rented out, which was empty. It came with a Greek Cypriot servant called Angelus, who looked after us all the time we were there, and his wife was our laundress. As our heavy baggage had not, by then, arrived he was extremely generous and lent us all that we needed to be able to move in.

We had bought ourselves a baby Fiat car, and had driven it across to Kyrenia. One day when I came back for lunch, I parked the Fiat outside our carob store but omitted to apply the handbrake fully. The car started to move down the steep slope towards the harbour, where it was stopped by a patrol of the Wiltshire Regiment, which was occupying the castle, and who managed to prevent it going into the sea, for which we were eternally grateful.

One of our first moves was to buy a suitable boat. Taking advice from the local fishermen, we bought ourselves a Felucca which we equipped with an outboard motor. Not being great sailors, we managed to sail our Felucca straight out of the harbour and back again without incident. This was very popular with the local fishermen, as the Royal Engineers, who had a sailing club at the west end of the harbour, were nervous about sailing in the strong westerly winds prevailing in northern Cyprus for most of the year. When the Royal Engineers saw us sailing, they followed

The author with his car in the hills above Kyrenia.

suit, but most of their yachts capsized outside the harbour and had to be rescued by the fishermen, at £5 per incident. Capsize we did not, and we kept our equilibrium, eventually gaining enough confidence to sail up and down the coast with impunity. When we left Cyprus all the fishermen lined up to buy our boat and we took the best offer for it.

The Turkish-Cypriot Harbourmaster, Jemal Figret, had an English wife called Sally who owned a beauty parlour in Kyrenia, in whom the Duke of Newcastle, who had a large yacht moored in the harbour, showed great interest. All the young officers used to come with their field glasses to watch the goings on and place bets as to with whom the Duke would leave. He finally sailed away with Sally, leaving Figret and their little son distraught. Also, living in Cyprus had been Lord Douro, now Duke of Wellington, who had been commanding the Blues and Royals. He was followed by the Honourable Julian Berry. When we got back to the England he was very generous, and frequently asked me to shoot at his estate at Hackwood.

On one of our excursions, we saw a sail, late in the evening, to the east of the harbour. Using our outboard motor, we were able to investigate. This mysterious sail turned out to be a yacht that had turned turtle, being sailed by the US Consul General. He and his wife and two little boys were soaked in sea water and very cold. We were able to bring them all into port and offer them hot baths and food. They were lucky to have been picked up by us, as the light had been fading.

Pamela was able to satisfy her love for entertaining in the carob store, in which we had a large open fire. We had frequent dinner parties and dances to the gramophone, at one of which Marcia Kendrew, the sixteen-year-old daughter of General Kendrew, who commanded the Army in Cyprus, was invited as there was a shortage of single girls. Lady Kendrew would only allow her to come if Michael Allenby, son of Field Marshall Lord Allenby and also ADC to the Governor of Cyprus, chaperoned her and ensured that she was back home by midnight, which of course she was not. At that party, she met her future husband, Richard Abel-Smith, the son of Lady May Abel-Smith, daughter of Princess Alice, Countess of Athlone.

Also I remember the times when the authorities would ring me with a map reference, to which Pamela had to drive me in the middle of the night, and return alone.

The Grenadier camp was outside Nicosia on the road to the Troodos Mountains, as was the camp of the Blues. As petrol was short, we used to take it in turns to take our cars, which meant that our wives always had transport. We used to go to Nicosia to get our supplies of wine from the Keo Depot. They had both red and white wines that came in two-gallon drums. There were various trades to be found along the road from Kyrenia, and a very good pottery and embroidery. On Sundays, we used take a picnic and go looking for partridges, but sadly no shooting was allowed.

The Harbour Club was run by Roy and Judy Finlay, and was a great place to dine in Kyrenia.

We had no problems with EOKA, and no intelligence that there would be, so altogether our time in Cyprus turned out to be a happy holiday. Despite that, trouble festered between the Greek and Turkish communities. These were finally settled by the security in Cyprus being taken over by the United Nations, a wise decision and the only way in which the Greeks and the Turks could happily cohabit.

13

Public Duties, 1957–58

On our return from Cyprus we bought a small house in London, 27 Hill Gate Place, W8, and I started public duties with the Queen's Company 1st Battalion Grenadier Guards. Public duties consisted of sleeping at Wellington Barracks, Buckingham Palace and the Tower of London, at which location I could have my dinner brought in by Pamela. She had to leave by 10p.m. In the middle of the night, I was alerted by the Sergeant of the Guard, who told me that a man had climbed the fence outside the guard room. I found the intruder hanging from a drain pipe – underneath was a guardsman's bayonet, about three inches from the man's rectum. I alerted the Metropolitan Police, and he was arrested.

During that summer I was appointed Adjutant of the Royal Tournament at Earls Court, a position which came with a number of free seats and a night in the royal box, at which we were able to entertain our friends after a dinner party. I had great difficulty trying to stop the naval cadets from climbing the rigging and getting level with the bathrooms in the flats adjoining Earl's Court and peeking at the girls. There were many complaints. Towards the end of the Royal Tournament I arranged to grease the wall where the rigging was in order to stop these activities.

When we went to garden parties at Buckingham Palace, Guardsman Nobes used to drive our car, and when all the notables were called forward on the loudspeaker, he was to be found in the forecourt in Buckingham Palace with his feet on the steering wheel reading a whodunit, so we had no waiting for our car.

After a spell of public duties, the Queen's Company travelled to Salisbury Plain for a month's annual autumn training. It was at this time King Hussein's cousin, King Faisal of Iraq, together with the Prime Minister, Nuri Sayed, and leading figures in the Government of Iraq were assassinated. General Sir Charles Jones, who had been Commandant of the Staff College during my term there, had been selected for the post of Secretary to the Baghdad Pact, and had asked for me as his PA, but all the plans had been changed as a result of Abd al Karim Qasim's military coup. King Hussein would have liked to have brought Glubb Pasha back to sort out this emergency, but he did not wish to go because he said he was too old, and 'Bromage is the man you want.'

As soon as I arrived at Salisbury Plain, the Commanding Officer's orderly came running up to me to say that the Lt

Colonel was on the telephone and wished to speak to me. He said 'The Chief of the Imperial General Staff would like you to go back to Jordan, immediately. Would you be prepared to go, you can have anything you like?' My reply was, 'Yes, if I can take my wife, my soldier servant, my spaniel and my guns.' I contacted Pamela with this news, and she sent a telegram to her old nanny, asking her to come up to London to look after her.

I decided that the best way to go was to fly to Beirut, and from there fly to Amman, although at that stage I had not realised that the US Marines were landing in the Lebanon. When all the air transport had been arranged, Guardsman Nobes and I joined the first available flight to Beirut, from where we hoped to catch a flight to Amman.

Six weeks later when I flew back from Jordan to collect Pamela and the spaniel, we got as far as Beirut. I found the Middle East again in turmoil following Qasim's opportunist revolution in Iraq, and the US Marines landing in the Lebanon to try and stop Hezbullah (The Party of God), which was trying to take over the country. I flew on to Amman, leaving Pamela and the spaniel in the St George Hotel, which ran out of food except for curried prawns and rice, on which they had to live for a few days. Beirut was under curfew, so the Defence Attaché, Colonel Alec Brodie, had visited Pamela every evening to see if she was happy. After a few days I collected them and we flew on to Amman.

That went well, but when we arrived at Beirut, we were met by Colonel Alec Brodie. His main worry was our spaniel,

Tin. Poor Tin was much-travelled, and in order to get into Lebanon, I had to get a certificate from the local Director of Veterinary Surgeons to say that he was inspected and found to be in good health and fit to enter the country. With the help of a few Lebanese pounds, the Veterinary Inspector got out of bed to certify that Tin had been inspected and was perfectly fit to enter the country, so we managed to get a flight to Amman armed with the certificate.

14

Amman, 1958

When I arrived at Amman, I found that nobody appeared to be expecting me. I contacted the Embassy and asked them to find suitable accommodation for me and my family, which they did at Jebal Luwebdi, which faced across the valley at our old Jordanian headquarters, near where Glubb Pasha had had his house.

I sent a telegram to the War Office to find out the rate of allowance for an unmarried unaccompanied guardsman, living out in Amman. All telegrams are signed by the Ambassador. Back came the answer, 'Who is Johnston? State his name, rank and number?' I replied, 'Johnston is HM Ambassador!' The Department was so embarrassed that all Guardsman Nobes's allowances were paid forthwith.

The house that the Embassy hired belonged to a Palestinian from Nablus. It stood at the edge of the valley, which was

The author with his spaniel Tin on his balcony at Amman.

being built up storey by storey up the hill. On top of the hill lived William Clark, who was the Director of UNRWA. Bill Clark had been a District Commissioner in the Sudan before World War II. He was a very erudite homosexual who became a close friend and bridge partner. He was extremely hospitable, and on our return from Azraq there was always a message sent over to say that he was expecting us for dinner. We always knew to expect fish and chips! Tinny always rushed in to dry and clean himself on Bill's Persian carpets. We shared a gardener called Yacoub. As the Palestinians cannot pronounce a hard 'C', he became 'Yaoub'. Yacoub looked after several gardens at the top of the hill, and if anybody needed new plants, he stole from the other gardens, so he was always well stocked and well off. One night there was a huge crash and our garden, which had been surrounded by a retaining wall above the wadi, suddenly collapsed.

One of the responsibilities of the Military Attaché's office was to look after the graveyard adjoining the airport. I asked Pamela to look after it. She had bulbs sent out from England in the diplomatic bag, and in the end the graveyard looked well maintained.

There was a tailor called Haik Peltekian, who made good tropical suits with red threads running through the cloth on the underside to deflect the sun. I still have one to this day.

While we were living in Amman, King Hussein escaped from an attempt on his life by the Syrian Air Force. It appeared that he was travelling to Europe in his own aeroplane, accompanied as co-pilot by Wing Commander Jock Dalgleish, who was commanding the Royal Air Force Mission. He was evidently overflying Syria without having informed the authorities. As a result, he was met by two MIG-17 fighters, which demanded that he landed in Syria. He handed the controls to Dalgleish, who turned round and returned to Amman. The King was eternally grateful to him for having saved his life.

Of course, once we were established, my thoughts turned to Azraq, where I had left my house some years before, so I asked the Royal Army Ordinance Corps to provide me with a Land Rover, which they kindly did from their vehicle park at

Mohamed Hashim's house at Azraq, leased to the author.

Aqaba, and which I kept for the rest of my tour. At the time I arrived the Embassy was in a state of mayhem because one of the senior Foreign Office officials, who subsequently reached the very pinnacle of his profession, went on holiday without remembering to give the combination of the locks to anybody else. The first thing that had to be done was to get into the secure offices in the Embassy, so the Political Officer was given the task of picking the locks, which he did competently until he came to the last box, in which all the keys for the Holy of Holies were kept. This eluded him, but the Military Attaché, a Royal Engineer with a fertile brain, took the box with the keys inside and threw it on the floor. It burst open and the keys were scattered everywhere, so the Embassy was in business again.

We were lucky enough to go to the midnight Christmas Service at the Church of the Nativity in Bethlehem in both

The author (second from left) with General Habis al Majali, Pamela and General Akash al Zebn at a reception at Amman.

1958 and 1959. Tickets were very hard to obtain, but being diplomats we were able to acquire them.

We were extremely concerned, because when I was told that I was to be Assistant Military Attaché I had visions of continuous entertaining, and so it was lucky that I had packed the family silver in a small leather suitcase, which, having gone astray, eventually landed up at Jerusalem Airport. We were very relieved to hear from the airport that a mysterious suitcase with our name on it had arrived there.

Our house was small and primitive, with no running hot water, so to get a bath with a few inches of hot water we had to put three bags of olive shucks, soaked in paraffin, into our Geyser. We had Damascus stoves which ran on paraffin to heat the house. We cooked on a three-burner paraffin stove, and washed up by using kettles. We rented

Qasr al Kharani.

our furniture and rugs from a dealer, named Faik Bisharat. Pamela had luckily brought out some material, which she had made up into curtains.

We had many visitors, and there was plenty for them to see and do. There was the Roman amphitheatre, Jerash, Irbid, Mafraq, Petra, Um al Quwain, Azraq, Jebel Druze, and H4 and H5 pumping stations on the old pipeline from Iraq to Haifa. Also, the Qasr al Kharani Omayid hunting lodge, outside Azraq, and the old ruin Qasr Halibat on the track to Azraq. Jerusalem was a two-night excursion every month, and we stayed at the American colony, owned by the Vesta family, and which enabled me to carry out my duties on the West Bank. On one of our visits Pamela went into the souk and bought one of the porter's baskets, which he carried on his head, as a bed for Tin. We put it in our bedroom. On the following day we found that Tin had been very badly bitten under his tail, and when we disinfected the basket, bed bugs emerged in large numbers and were climbing up the walls. That problem had to be dealt with immediately. There were also the Palestinian potteries, which produced turquoise glass and distinctive pottery. There were embroiderers as well, from whom anything could be ordered.

One of our frequent visitors was the Queen's Messengers, who came every week to Amman and whom the diplomats were reluctant to entertain because of their allowances. They had their uses, taking and bringing odd things home and out to us!

There was plenty of shooting, including quail in the late spring in the Jordan Valley, and we shot partridges in September at Bir al Debaghat in the Shera Mountains west of Maan. We used to set up camp each autumn, and Sir Leonard Figg, the First Secretary, and later our ambassador in Dublin, usually accompanied us.

After one of our fishing trips on our way back from Aqaba to Amman, we rescued a lorry driver who had run out of petrol. Little did we know that we would meet again when our driver Abuzaid fell asleep at the wheel of the car, which then ran off the road into a wadi. Our friend the lorry driver, who was passing at the time, kindly rescued us and took us and our spaniel back to Amman, leaving Abuzaid with the car, which was recovered the next day.

In the early spring of 1960 I was aware of pains in my abdomen, so I got in touch with our London doctor,

The author (on right) being received at the Palace.

Christopher Grandage, who arranged for me to visit a well-known specialist called Arthur Dowthwaite. So we took some leave and returned to the United Kingdom for the appointment. It was discovered that I had a duodenal ulcer, which meant living on slops and bed rest. It also emerged that my wife, Pamela, was expecting a baby, so we were able to make some advanced plans for the expected birth. We interviewed a number of contenders for the posts of maternity nurse and nanny, and bought all the necessary gear, unavailable locally. The family treasure cot was done up, and we were lucky to have all the baby clothes we needed. Unfortunately, when we arrived at Marseilles the train door opened, and the pram and its contents finished up on the railway line! We were able to recover it in time to board our ship.

At that stage Sir Charles Johnston was appointed Governor of Aden, and left us for that colony. The Foreign Office started to worry about my security and that of the new child we were expecting. Our driver used to put my Browning automatic pistol underneath Pamela's pillow so that she was able to look after our security at night. I put it around among my Bedouin friends that we needed a security guard, and I thought the best place for him to live would be in the garage of our house. There was no way in which Her Majesty's Government would have paid for a necessary guard, so I approached various sheikhs, who were my friends, to provide a guard who would stay with us until after the baby was born. The result of this was the emergence of Qitab, a slave of one of the sheikhs of Dahamsha, a sub-tribe of Anezeh which inter-married with the Ruwala. This was a satisfactory arrangement, provided it never emerged in an official document that we were employing a slave as a security guard. It did not, and the whole understanding worked out satisfactorily until our eventual departure from Jordan. The new Ambassador, who replaced Charles Johnston, was the Hon. John Henniker-Major, who presented his credentials in Amman at about the time that our son was born. His wife was a Canadian, Osla. Jordan was a popular post in the Foreign Office at that time, and Osla could see a crisis appearing over the forthcoming birth of our child. Pamela, who hated hospitals, which anyway did not exist, was determined that the baby should be born at home despite the potential lack of medical cover. We were bombarded with telegrams from the United Kingdom urging us to return in time for the birth, including a very long telegram from my mother-in-law. Pamela was adamant that the baby should be born in Amman. Apart from anything else, we had a multitude of Bedouins wishing us well. If the child had been a girl, all would be disappointed, and Pamela would have hidden her under the bed!

As luck would have it, a boy emerged after a period of nail-biting delay! The joy that followed the announcement of the birth of a male child was considerable. During the delay, the maternity nurse had bitten her nails up until the time of the birth. There was relief and jubilation all round. Queues of Bedouins and diplomats formed to see the new baby, who was firmly tucked up at Pamela's side so no one could touch him. Everyone had to take their turn. At eleven o'clock the maternity nurse said, 'No more visitors today,' but back they came the next day. They always brought live chickens, rabbits, sheep and gold coins for him, and dropped them by his bath. Pamela found it quite a performance to change over the gold from the treasure cot to the pram, which occurred every morning. This continued for some while, until Nanny came out. Pamela went to the airport to meet the aeroplane, which arrived in the early hours of the morning. This all took place after the assassination of the Prime Minister, in which members of the Husseini family had been implicated. They had been condemned to death, and by Turkish custom they had been hanged at dawn in red tunics. When Pamela and Nanny returned to Amman, our driver drove round the square so that our newly arrived Nanny could see the murderers hanging in red tunics from the scaffold. We had been pressed to have a celebratory party, and we decided that it should take place at Azraq, in the desert some forty miles east of Amman. One of the most vociferous celebrators was Mohamed Eyad, who had been orderly to Norman Lash, until his death.

I rented a small house at Azraq, in which I slept when I was shooting. It was owned by the head of the Badia Police. Before my marriage, I had painted all the ceiling beams and built a mud-brick annexe for use as a kitchen. I had also built a mud-brick hut open on one side on top of an unsuccessful well, which produced no water but a strong smell of sulphur.

Celebrating the birth of the author's son at a party at Azraq.

On this I had built a loo with a polished mahogany seat, which we named 'a loo with a view', as it looked out over a graveyard and open desert. After we were married, I did some serious shooting. In our hut, we had two beds and a few rudimentary chairs.

This house at Azraq was duly prepared, but it was too small to accommodate the number of potential celebrators, so we decided to feed everyone in the open. Mohamed Eyad managed to collect enough Bedouin cooks, most of whom had been in the Jordanian Army or Desert Police. We bought enough rams and sacks of rice, and borrowed a number of cooking pots from our Bedouin friends. I already had a tray on a stand to feed a large number of guests, which had given good service. Our final party took place at Azraq. The unfortunate rams were duly slaughtered, and all the guests provided for, and enough black Bedouin tents were erected to shelter the feast from the rays of the winter sun.

Many of our guests, from far and wide, brought with them their falcons, which sat on their swivels on their cars. Unfortunately, our baby was unable to come because Nanny thought the desert track was too rough for him at only six weeks old. We had a second party for diplomats and European visitors at our house in Amman.

Owing to the uncertainty of the length of my appointment, we had been unable to let our house in London. In the end, we had been in Amman for three happy years.

15

Excursions, 1958

S aid Malhas, the Land Rover agent in Jordan, sold us an aging second-hand Buick, in which we used to travel regularly to Beirut via the Syrian border and through Zahle. In Beirut we always stayed at the Normandy Hotel, where we met our old friends Kim Philby, Theo Larsen and many others. We used to bring all our rations and any drink that we required back to Jordan in the boot of the Buick. The only difficulties we experienced were when there were problems between Syria and Lebanon, involving the armies of both countries. It so happened on one occasion that Pamela wanted to relieve herself just after we had reached the Syrian border, at which point half the Syrian Army descended upon her, leaving her little time to pull up her pants and make it back to the car! Otherwise, we had no difficulty with either side.

When travelling to Beirut, or through Syria, I always made a point of wearing a tidy suit and brown felt hat. For some reason the hat must have had some influence on how we were received, both in Syria and in the Lebanon. I imagine that some French dignitaries in past times had worn similar hats. In any case, it eased our passage through both borders.

We used to stop in Damascus for lunch, where we used to visit the Souk al Hamadieh. On one of our visits, when my mother-in-law was staying with us, she went to relieve herself in the Sheraton Hotel and managed to lock herself into the loo, from which we had great difficulty in extracting her. We laughed our heads off, but she never saw the joke! The souk was full of surprises, one of which was that a number of antique Ming and Ching porcelain bowls and plates which had been built into the walls of the old houses, and when these were demolished they emerged, occasionally, without damage, and were sold in the souk very cheaply.

From Damascus we headed to Zahle, where we stopped for tea. The Foreign Office used to buy their duty-free alcohol for entertaining through a firm called Seconni & Speed, and no doubt still do. We found this expensive, so we used to buy the local Lebanese wine Ksara, red and white, and Taval rosé which are excellent. You could buy everything you needed in Beirut. We often dined at the Lucallus Restaurant, and went on to the Casino, reputed to have the best cabaret in the world. It was sadly closed down when it caught fire in the revolution of Hezbullah. We always drove our guests to see them off in Beirut, stopping for a short time in Damascus and Zahle en route. We used to spend a night at the Normandy Hotel to be able to see them off the next day.

On one occasion when we were away in England, Abdul Fatah, the son of our cook, took it into his head to take the Buick and drive it. He drove it into a wall and smashed it to pieces, so we had to find a replacement car we could use for our trips, as the other cars belonged to the Government. We replaced it with a Mercedes, which was equally satisfactory.

On one of our leaves we went from Kuwait to Verbier for a month's skiing holiday, as our house in London had been let, and it gave the children a great chance to learn to ski with the ski school in the morning and private lessons in the afternoon. On one such occasion, my six-year-old daughter dropped one of her battens when she was going up in the lift. Being rather mean and foreseeing problems with the ski shop, I went down in the evening in my pyjamas to retrieve the offending batten. The following morning, I had thick lumps in both thighs. Pamela insisted on calling the doctor, who referred me to his consultant, who they called *Herr Professor Doctor*. This gentleman came to see me, and sucked his teeth and said he could not understand what the problem was. I remarked, 'Could it be frostbite?' at which point he sounded as if he had found the Holy Grail, and said 'Ah ah, I diagnose frostbite in both thighs.' The swellings disappeared with time.

Tehran was another place to which we used to go, staying at the Park Hotel, where we met Peter Stirling, who had been with the Embassy. We also searched for and bought caviar. The bazaar was a great place to which we went from time to time to eat chelo kebab. We flew to Isphan, with its beautiful minarets and rose gardens. On one occasion when we flew on an internal flight from Isphan to Shiraz, the door fell off the aeroplane! The pilot carried on as if nothing had happened. It was very cold, with snow on the mountain-tops. Shiraz is a great place, and we found lovely rugs and carpets there.

Our leaves were mainly spent in England, breaking our journeys by disembarking in various different places, one of which was Lausanne, where we stayed in the Beau Rivage Hotel. The only accommodation available was a ground-floor suite with intercommunicating doors which King Saud had vacated that day. When we were dining, the head waiter came up to us and told us that our children had climbed out of the window. Pamela went back and put them to bed.

Abdul Aziz bin Abdul Mehsin Al Tuwaigary encouraged his trusted friend Hasan Shebib, a Palestinian, to organise a visit to Moscow for us. We were escorted around the Kremlin and various other places by a woman whom we suspected of being a Government official. On our last day we were able to find the best rug dealer, and bought five antique rugs. Hasan squared the customs, as antiques were not officially allowed to leave the country. We then went on to Czechoslovakia, where Hasan had an interest in a glass-manufacturing business which supplied glass to Saudi Arabia. We were extremely lucky, as he was able to get us a very favourable rate of exchange, which enabled us to buy table glasses, but it took a long time, as the shops shut their doors every half hour, which meant going backwards and forwards to be able to collect a set. We bought extra cheap suitcases for all the glass. Hasan had a friend who worked in the customs authority, which enabled us to pass glass through customs without problem.

Pamela always collected me from the Embassy so as to get to Azraq for the evening shooting, with Tinny and everything on board, followed by the staff car with cook and driver. We were very comfortable. We had a paraffin refrigerator and stove. We were often joined by Sir Leonard Figg. He slept in the Embassy hut, and used to join us for meals. To this day, he has never forgotten the time when he asked at what time he should come to dinner. Pamela said, 'Quarter to eight for eight'! A very nice Bostonian, Mel Johnson, used to join us, but seldom hit anything.

After I had been ill with the ulcer, we put in the largest tin laundry tub, and heated the hot water on a four-headed primus so that I was able to have a hot bath after my return from the birds' morning flight. The house was looked after by Mohamed Khalouf during the week, who filled up all our water tubs so that they were ready for the weekends. On and off, we spent many happy weekends there.

Azraq is an oasis at the head of the Wadi Sirhan. To the north and east of it are the lava belt, and to the south there are salt flats covering a relatively large area. The Druze village had been the resting place of T.E. Lawrence during the First World War. There is a Desert Police force just outside the Chechen village. The Transjordan Frontier Force had had a corrugated iron building which had reverted to the use

Captain in the Bardia Police at Azraq.

of the British Embassy at Amman. Unfortunately, it was seldom used by the Embassy's staff, but was therefore useful for some of our guests. All well-known breeds of duck used to migrate to Azraq, in addition to a large number of snipe, so it became a shooter's paradise. Max Graham used to join me there whenever he had the opportunity.

Teal and gargany are the first to arrive on the annual migration. The snipe and the odd woodcock arrive simultaneously. A little later on, the mallard, gadwall, pintail, widgeon, shoveler and pochard come. The bulk of them stay and leave again in the spring, some to Egypt, others to Iraq. Accompanying the migration are numerous harriers, which kill as many of the migrants as they can. I hate harriers. These evil birds come in four different varieties: hen, pallid, montague's and marsh. I made a point of killing every one I saw, remembering what they had done to the Duke of Buccleuch's Langham Moors, where for some extraordinary reason they were allowed to remain by the then Lord Dalkeith, and where they not only attacked the grouse but also killed every other bird in the area, including larks and pipits. What the RSPB do not seem to realise is that there are other inhabitants of heather as well as grouse. The red grouse is one of the world's rarest birds, as it is confined to the British Isles. One gets the impression that the RSPB dislike grouse. What has saved grouse is that they are excellent flyers, and difficult to shoot, in addition to being delicious to eat. On the other hand, harriers kill every other bird, particularly in the nesting season.

The migrating birds were invaluable for all the entertaining that I had to do as Assistant Military Attaché. Sir Alan Munro, who was an old childhood friend of Pamela's, came to me when he was at Shemlan on an Arabic course. I suggested that he should stay at our house in Azraq for six months, as we never used the house in the summer and he would never hear English spoken. Sadly, he had to return home, as he contracted amoebic dysentery.

One of the most interesting sights was to see the camels in their hundreds watering at Azraq. Also, when the locusts swarmed we used to take them back to Amman to fry and use as cocktail snacks.

Having read many of Major C.S. Jarvis's books, after he was Governor of Sinai, I was very interested in Aqaba, to

Watering camels at Azraq.

which I went after my companions were murdered by the Israelis when I was training the Palestine Supernumerary Police. Originally, when I first went to Aqaba, I stayed at the Government Guest House. There I met Radwan Hasan, who had been Major Jarvis's boatman. Radwan was a great fisherman. Unfortunately, he had lost a number of his fingers when throwing explosives into the water to kill bait with which to catch the bigger fishes. We started to go to Aqaba quite regularly, and I always contacted Radwan in advance. On one of my first visits, we had a picnic on the shore of the Gulf of Aqaba, where we met a certain Emir Abdullah Sudairi, who was also picnicking with his wife and infant son. He had come into the Gulf of Aqaba from the Red Sea Littoral, but I never knew where he was based. I suspect it was in the area of Yenbo. The Sudairis are a well-known family in Saudi Arabia, where they occupy various positions of authority. The Emira is a charming lady from Aleppo in Syria. The ladies from Aleppo are both beautiful and intelligent, and we soon formed a friendship. We were able to reciprocate their hospitality when they visited us in Amman shortly afterwards.

Radwan and his brother Mohamed are very experienced fishermen who know every inch of the Gulf of Aqaba, from the ruined Crusader castle on the western side of the Gulf, which dates back to Reynald de Châtillon, back to the port and out to Tiran Island at the mouth of the Gulf. History tells us that Raynald had been a real pirate and had been captured and presented to Salah al Din Ayoub, who refused the customary ransom and had him instantly killed.

On the tops of the coral reefs the crayfish fed at night. We used to go round with a pressure lamp, and when we saw one, pick it up and put it into a sack. They were extremely painful creatures, because they always scratched us with their long feelers and with the prickles on their backs. Occasionally we stopped to have a brew up and boil them alive to bring back to Amman. We caught a great many fish of various varieties, including a blue tunny, which I hooked in the middle of the Gulf, and barracuda, which are prevalent on both sides. We also caught a large number of groupers, some of which were quite big and which always caused problems,

Radwan Hasan and Pamela in his boat at Aqaba.

as they tended to dive into the coral reefs, where they often managed to break our lines before we could recover them. We loved the fishing, and were keen to go to Aqaba whenever we could. Later on when Sam Spiegel, was filming *Lawrence of Arabia* and was based at Maan, we used to take senior members of the directing staff to fish with us. They always came back pleased, with enough fish and crayfish to feed as many staff as they could manage. We had to be a little careful and wear gym shoes when fishing, as some of the fish had poisonous spines, which could cause agony for those unlucky enough to stand on one. We encouraged others to go to Aqaba, which caused some jealousy on occasions, as they insisted on using either Radwan or Mohamed's boats, so we always had to book one of them in advance of our arrival and obtain visas to visit the Saudi coast. I had to be a little cautious, as the Foreign Office was rather circumspect about our relations with the Saudis at that time, but no real problems ever occurred.

Radwan's family have transformed Aqaba and become very prosperous, and are now owners of a good many shops and properties in the village, while maintaining their interests in fishing. We never envisaged at the time just how popular Aqaba would become for tourists, particularly from Scandinavia.

16

Sam Spiegel's Film:
Laurence of Arabia, 1959

Before I left the United Kingdom, Charles Johnston asked me if I would pay special attention to the needs of a well-known film producer named Sam Spiegel, who was due to go out to Jordan to arrange to film *Lawrence of Arabia*, and to grant him any help that he might need. It turned out that they had already shot half the film in Morocco. This was at a time of unrest, when the loyalty of various senior officers in the Arab Legion was in question, following Abu Nuwar's unsuccessful attempt at a revolution. At about this time, after the massacre of the royal family in Iraq, both the Foreign Office and the Ministry of Defence were worried that something similar might happen in Jordan. As a result, and because much of the Iraqi Army was still in the Mafraq area, the problem was a difficult one diplomatically. The Parachute Brigade was sent to land at Amman. The landing took place without incident. The Brigade Commander was Brigadier, subsequently General, Thomas Pearson. Attached to Brigade Headquarters was the Brigadier, subsequently Major General, E.V.M Strickland, who had been the Commander of an armoured-car regiment in the Arab Legion.

The Ambassador's wife, Natasha, was staying with the Hultons of *Picture Post* fame. Before their marriage, Natasha had been Natasha Begratzien, and she had married Charles during the war. The Begratziens had been Kings of Georgia, and were very much involved in the politics of the Middle East. At that time, Natasha's mother was Abbess of the Russian Convent in Jerusalem. Having duly contacted Natasha, I stayed at the Residence, in Amman until Charles's return to Jordan. During my time at the Residency, locals were reluctant to visit, so when Charles returned I asked to move to my own house. I was looked after by the famous 'Mo', who had been, in a previous incarnation in Cairo during the War, the servant of the Stirling brothers. While the Johnstons stayed in the Middle East, Peter Stirling eventually returned to the Diplomatic Service. I subsequently met him in Tehran when Pamela and I had visited the Iranian capital to look for antique rugs. David Stirling resuscitated some elements of the Long Range Desert Group. I met him a number of times in London, where he was working as an unofficial advisor to the Special Air Service.

Where I was useful to Sam Spiegel was in the recruitment of tribesmen to help as extras in the film he was making. The provision of Howeitat tribesmen was of great assistance to Sam and, as many of the tribesmen had no other employment, they were very happy to work with the film. So the film helped the interior security of Jordan and kept everyone busy; too busy to be involved in local politics. In fact, the difficulties over the loyalty of individual officers did not emerge in the south of Jordan, where the Bedouins gave their full support to the royal family, so the film served to cement the Howeitat and remove any worry about them during this particularly delicate time.

The Defence Attaché at Amman was Colonel Aitkin Lawrie. Unfortunately, the officers of the Parachute Brigade, for some reason, felt that the Defence Attaché was not of great help to them during the time of their landing. This was most unfortunate, as Aitkin did all he could to help the Brigade, but the impression was left, and no doubt reported to London that Aitkin had not helped as much as he might have done. I did my best to defend Aitkin, who was a brilliant officer and to my mind had done all he could to facilitate the landing of the Brigade at Amman. Fortunately, my presence at Amman kept me free to work as I wished with the Howeitat. I had a close rapport with Sam Spiegel and the various administrative directors of the film. I had no experience of the administration required when a film was being made, but I was obviously useful not only in arranging provision of extras but in ironing out minor disputes which arose on the administrative side. Spiegel asked me to take part in the film, but for obvious reasons I declined. We used to have great parties for the actors and the administrative staff at our house in Amman. David Lean and his Indian wife and Peter O'Toole, who played Lawrence, also enjoyed our hospitality. We went on a fishing trip to Aqaba, and the administrative director bought our entire catch, to our great satisfaction.

When we were finally due to leave, Sam Spiegel offered us the use of his yacht, for all that I had done to help with the film. It had a crew of 27, and was anchored at Aqaba, but it was not to be, because our Scottish nanny refused to allow our six-month-old baby on board because it had no medical facilities. Tipping a crew would have been quite a problem.

When the film was finished, we were invited to the premier in London.

At about this time Colonel Charles Chaplin took over from Colonel Aitkin Lawrie as Military Attaché in Jordan. One of the duties of the Military Attaché was to reconnoitre the roads in Jordan, which mainly consisted of the roads running north to south, either straight south to Maan or across the hills via Kerak, Tafileh and Shobek, thence to Ras al Negb and Aqaba.

At that time it was mid-winter. Pamela and I decided it would be a good time to visit Aqaba to do some fishing. It also gave me a chance to see how the new road was progressing. We set off in our Land Rover, with our driver, Mohamed Irkab. We spent a happy week at Aqaba and caught some fish, but as we turned north to go home to Amman, I decided to go up the mountain road, rather than follow the railway line from Maan to Amman.

The sky was lowering when we set off, and I warned Pamela that we might meet snow on the Shera Mountains. Sure enough we did. The snow started to get deeper and deeper as we reached the same level as Shobek, so I decided that we should go no further. We were about level with Wadi Musa and Petra when we got well and truly stuck in a very deep twenty-foot snowdrift, but I managed to walk down to Wadi Musa police station, where I got the sergeant in charge to find enough labourers to help dig our vehicle out, but obviously even after that obstacle was overcome, the weather prevented us from going further, so we slept at the police station. We spent eight nights there, sleeping on camp beds with wet horse blankets. We existed on tins of sardines and tomato puree made into soup with Carnation milk, and bread which was made in the village. Luckily, we had two hot-water bottles and two primus stoves, which enabled us to keep warm. Poor Pamela had a difficult time, as the police sergeant had to open the gates of the police station to let her out, from time to time, for normal sanitation. No one in Amman knew where we were, so we were reported missing to the Ministry in London.

Eventually, help arrived from Amman in the shape of the King's helicopter, which I helped land on the village football ground using my shamag (head cloth). We were flown out to Maan while our poor driver had to follow on horseback. He fell off his horse en route, and broke his gold teeth. I subsequently tried to claim their cost from the War Office (as it then was) in London, but had no satisfactory answer. Eventually our helpers from Wadi Musa were paid. Our Land Rover and driver joined us a month later. When we arrived back in Amman, the price of paraffin had risen from one to five dinars per jerry can. It had been very cold.

17

Saudi Arabia, 1961–63

Having returned from Jordan, our small house was not suitable for a pram, and too small for us all. My uncle, Thomas Hawksley, promised us his father's house at number 56 Ladbroke Grove, which at the time had 36 Poles squatting in it. He paid to evict them. In order to do the renovations, we made the basement into a self-contained flat and let it on a 51-year trust lease. Our first and only tenant was Janet Foster.

The autumn of 1962 found me serving as a Staff Officer at Headquarters Eastern Command. It was a convenient posting for me, as we were able to live in our London house. Our son Charles was then two years old.

I was just starting a new appointment as Deputy Assistant Adjutant General in Headquarters Eastern Command when I received a telephone call from St John Armitage, who was in London. St John asked me to make a list of staff officers who would be suitable to serve on a mission to the Saudi Arabian National Guard. I lobbied one or two of my friends on the staff, and asked them if they would be prepared to serve in Saudi Arabia. That was as far as it went at that stage, then St John changed his tack and asked for help to draw up suitable terms of service for a mission to go to Saudi Arabia.

Those responsible at the Arabian Department had been slightly uncertain as to what had actually been requested. Was it to be a large mission or a small one? Were the members to remain on loan, or as seconded officers, or were they required to retire from British service and to go on contract to the National Guard? In any case, was I prepared, in principle, to volunteer for service for the mission? My answer to the last question was a 'Yes', and it was agreed, with the Department, that there should be a preliminary visit to discover what would be needed, and to suggest suitable terms under which a mission might serve. Subsequently, it was decided that Brigadier Tim Hope Thompson and I should go out on a preliminary visit.

Tim had been commanding the Proof and Experimental Establishment at Chertsey in Surrey. He should have been a General, but ill-luck had blighted his career. He commanded the Indian Airborne Brigade in the early days of the War when the Japanese advanced on the Indian border through Burma. Tim's brigade was thrown in, piecemeal, to stem the advance, and was severely defeated before the front was stabilised. He had a nervous breakdown and returned to the United Kingdom to recover. Subsequently, he commanded a battalion of Royal Scots Fusiliers in Northern Europe, where he distinguished himself. In the 1950s he became GSO1 of the Arab Legion Division in Jordan, where I came to know him and admire his capabilities. Then, after subsequent staff appointments, he commanded the Scottish Lowland Brigade at Glasgow. His appointment to the Proof and Experimental Establishment indicated he would not be promoted Major General.

Tim stayed the night in our London house. The next day Pamela, who was expecting our second child, drove us to London Airport in the pouring rain in my aging Hillman shooting brake with the bulk of our luggage on the roof. When we reached about half way, the rack holding the luggage slipped off. Fortunately, there was no damage and we were able to complete our journey to Heathrow, from where we had booked a flight to Rome. It was an inauspicious start.

On reaching Rome, we checked in at a smart hotel, booked for us by the Saudi Ambassador. The following morning we called upon him, rather surprisingly at the Chancellery, which was closed, so we were ushered into the Ambassador's office, where we produced our passports, which were stamped personally by him. He was soon afterwards transferred to London to succeed Hafedh al Wahba, who had been Ambassador in post in London until diplomatic relations were broken because of problems over the Buraimi Oasis in 1952.

On the following day, we flew to Jeddah, where we were met by one of Kemal Adham's staff, and housed in the Jeddah

Palace Hotel. Kemal was a member of the Emir's entourage. The hotel, rather run-down, was owned by Abdullah Suliman. Despite the cockroaches, we were comfortable enough. The next morning we had an audience with Crown Prince Faisal bin Abdul Aziz at his palace, and met Amr Saqaf, the Wakil, at the Ministry of Foreign Affairs, who was de facto Foreign Minister while the Emir Faisal was Head of the Council of Ministers. We also called on Frank Brenchley, Chargé d'Affaires, at the British Embassy, now reopened after the breach in diplomatic relations. Frank was a high-class diplomat who had come from Khartoum, temporarily, where he was Counsellor at the Embassy.

Emir Faisal was charming and erudite. Although he spoke English extremely well, having visited Great Britain many times over the previous forty years, he only communicated in his own language, avoiding any chance of a mistake. Once the audience was over, we returned to our hotel. That evening, Kemal entertained us to dinner, where we met many new friends.

The following morning we flew to Riyadh for an audience with the Emir Abdullah bin Abdul Aziz, the newly appointed Commander of the National Guard. Kemal came with us to introduce us to His Royal Highness, now King, Abdullah bin Abdul Aziz. The latter seemed rather surprised to see us, as he had no formal warning of our visit. He had, at that time, a pronounced impediment in his speech, which subsequently disappeared in the course of time, but was quite alarming to members of his staff, particularly when he was angry, as when he started to stutter they had no idea of what would come out next. In the Emir's ante-room was Hamed al Hamoudi, his private secretary, and Mohamed bin Trad al Shalan of the Sotam, a sub-tribe of the Ruawla, acting as his Assistant Secretary. Also, in an annexe to the secretariat sat Ibrahim al Husaini, a Syrian who had been Chief of Police in Damascus until he was sent into exile with the change of government. Another Syrian, Madhafer Jazary, who claimed to have been an officer in the Syrian Air Force, shared Ibrahim's office downstairs. We were escorted downstairs to be introduced to Abdul Aziz Al Tuwaigary, the deputy for the National Guard. He equated to a permanent secretary, and was at the same time second-in-command to the Emir Abdullah. He had little English, so Kemal acted as interpreter for Tim during our visit. What amazed Tim was the Wakil's squint, which was so pronounced that one eye appeared to point at ninety degrees from the other. For a visitor who did not know which was the good eye, this was most disconcerting. I was impressed by the Wakil's quick mind and relaxed attitude, but Kemal told us, as we left, that Faisal would have liked a bad report on Abdul Aziz, as he did not know him and did not trust him. When we left the National Guard Headquarters, we offered Ibrahim a lift back to the hotel, which was indeed the only hotel, the other having been taken over by the Saudi Ministry of Defence to house the US Army Mission. He left his file behind in our car, and I picked it up, meaning to return it to him, but Tim took it from me, saying that he

111

would read its contents before returning it. I was angry and embarrassed, but failed to persuade him to give it back immediately. In fact, the file held nothing but Army tactics copied from an army training manual. Ibrahim knew he had it. Tim returned it to him next morning, but his ill-mannered act soured my relationship with Ibrahim for a year before we got to know each other better, and built a relationship on mutual trust. I became a source of Havana cigars, of which he was inordinately fond.

The next day we had another audience with Emir Abdullah before returning to Jeddah. Kemal, who knew that I was fond of fishing, arranged for a coastguard launch to be available at the creek, at the north of the town. I only caught two small fish, but had a happy day on the Red Sea while Tim started work on our report.

On the following day, we paid a farewell call on the Crown Prince. In the absence of any convenient flight, we flew back to London on Olympic Airlines, via Athens. On the way, Tim and I made a draft of the terms of service recommended for members of a potential British mission to the National Guard. Our key recommendation was that the mission should be paid by Saudi Arabia, and the costs subsequently recovered from Her Majesty's Government. In that way any potential arguments over costs could be avoided, and members of the mission would be free of British Income Tax, an incentive that we estimated would attract the necessary quality of volunteers. As I expected to be a member of the mission, a degree of self-interest had been involved. The draft terms of service was accepted by the Ministry of Defence in London and tacitly by Amr Saqaf, the Deputy of the Saudi Ministry of Foreign Affairs. Although the memorandum of understanding on this subject between the two Governments was actually never signed on the Saudi side, the terms of service, worked out in the back of an aging Greek Comet, stood the test of time. They are still extant today, with some modifications.

I did not see Tim for some months, as he went to Scotland at the end of his tour at Chertsey. He retired the following year (1964) and became Commandant of the Queen Victoria College at Dunblane, where he died several years later. An unlucky officer who might well have been a general if the timing had been right for him.

Emir Abdullah bin Abdul Aziz was in Jeddah, as it was early summer and the important Saudi princes move with their families down to Jeddah from Riyadh to avoid the heat, although the discomfort of the furnace-like heat of the area around the capital was by no means worse than the damp heat of the Red Sea Littoral. When we arrived, we had some problems, as various accommodation and amenities promised by the Saudi negotiator did not materialise.

One of the first tasks given to me was to secure the National Guard ammunition depot, north of Riyadh. I re-wired the door to the ammunitions depot and made it as secure as possible, but having done that I had a look at the contents of the depot. As the Saudis never wrote off any unwanted, unused or damaged ammunition, some was very old, and in a dangerous state, and we were faced with the problem of how to destroy it. We summoned the help of the Royal Army Ordnance Corp Ammunition Inspectorate from the United Kingdom to destroy as much as possible of the outdated ammunition, which included a large quantity of Stokes mortar rounds, the boxes of which were stamped 'British Expeditionary Force 1916'. In some cases the explosives had crystallised and run out of the huts in which they were housed. They managed to clear the most hazardous explosives and destroy them in the desert to the north of Riyadh.

By then I was joined by a colonel of the Blues and Royals named Kenneth Timbrell, who unfortunately had no great gift for the Arabic language. As a result, he had difficulty in putting his views across to the officers of the National Guard, and although he struggled on bravely, he eventually had nervous problems. He was a useful member of the Mission, until retired hurt.

One of things that he arranged was that the National Guard would equip itself with an early wire-guided anti-tank missile called Vigilant, produced by Vickers, which provided a small team of technicians to introduce Vigilant and oversee the initial training of suitable operators. Personally, I was always suspicious of Vigilant, probably because of an innate conservatism, which did not help me to assimilate the whole concept of ground-to-ground missiles. The initial training of operators appeared to be going satisfactorily, and a demonstration was arranged in the desert north of Riyadh. The demonstration was attended by King Faisal bin Abdul Aziz as well as Prince Abdullah (now King Abdullah bin Abdul Aziz), but it ran into unforeseen problems at an early stage when the missiles being demonstrated all crashed into the desert unexpectedly without travelling very far. It emerged that the static electricity over the desert affected the wire by which the missiles were guided. I was one of the few senior members of the National Guard who called on Prince Abdullah that evening to discuss the day's events. We were all anxious about how the Emir would react to the fiasco, but we need not have worried, because the Emir talked to the King, who said to him that this sort of thing happened with missiles and had drawn a comparison with the problems experienced at Cape Canaveral. So instead of the expected umbrage, the failure was assigned to experimentation.

One of the main influences on the Saudi side was the Wakil in the Foreign Ministry. I had great difficulty in getting him to accept the Mission, but he did so with personal charm, and in the end I think that he could be considered one of the moving lights in the establishment of the National Guard. I asked the Emir if I could select a number of officers of Saudi tribal origin, and suggested that they be offered the chance to volunteer for service in the National Guard. He accepted, and I drew up a list of suitable Bedouin officers. I had been in touch with most of them over the years. They included General Saleh Deham, whom I knew well and who had served with me.

The Wakil of the National Guard was Abdul Aziz Al Tuwaigary, who acted as the main filter between Emir Abdullah and the various departmental heads. Abdul Aziz had a happy knack of listening to all applicants and of deciding instantly whether their applications were sound and could be channelled to the Emir.

Emir Abdullah, now King Abdullah, is a great Commander. He has a wicked sense of humour and an ability to switch his temper to become quite fierce when things go wrong. He has a most attractive personality, and anyone who has served with him has learnt to enjoy his humour. His appointment to command the National Guard was made by King Faisal before the latter's assassination, from his wide-ranging knowledge of the Saudi royal family and through his responsibility for advancing those who were of most value to the Kingdom.

All in the Kingdom of Saudi Arabia were shocked when King Faisal bin Abdul Aziz was assassinated by his nephew, the son of Emir Masaid, who imagined that he had a blood feud against the King because his brother was killed by the Saudi police. He was mentally unstable through an addiction to drugs. The murderer was beheaded on the orders of Prince Fahad bin Abdul Aziz, the Interior Minister, and that chapter was closed.

I did not hear a word from the Foreign Office or the Ministry of Defence for some time, but was informed by a friend that the Officer in Command was to be a Colonel K.F. Timbrell, a cavalry officer whom I had not met and about whom I knew nothing. He had been with the Trucial Oman Scouts, and lived in the Yemama Hotel. Eventually he became unwell and had to be evacuated. Time dragged on, and it became apparent that there was an obstacle to my appointment. I reckoned that probably it was Timbrell, but I could see no reason, as I had never met him.

Eventually, at the end of June, my posting to Saudi Arabia duly arrived. The letting agent for our London house was Bernard Walsh, who introduced as tenants first Dirk Bogarde, who kept it in immaculate order, and then Frank Zappa, who was an indifferent tenant. After that the tenancy went to a Saudi Royal Prince, for whom the Embassy paid all damages. After we had left the country, the agent's inventory clerk managed to fall through the trap door into the cellar from the dining-room, and broke his back.

As we had been warned to be prepared for any eventuality, Pamela and I decided to travel by sea. We found that a direct sailing to Jeddah was nigh unobtainable. However, accommodation was duly arranged on the Hansa Line ship MV *Stotzenfelz*, which was due to leave Rotterdam in late July. We took with us Hasan, our Sudanese servant, who travelled out via Harwich and the Hook of Holland, with our baggage, which amounted to 20 packing cases and 20 pieces of luggage. Hasan succeeded our previous servant, who went to be butler to the Jordanian Ambassador in Tehran. I agreed to release him on condition that he found a suitable replacement. He brought Hasan, who was a butler to Yusef Al Ghanem, a prominent Kuwaiti merchant who had a house in London. When I rang Yusef for a reference, he told me that Hasan was excellent but had contacted a venereal disease in London, and that as a result Yusef's wife had insisted on his departure. Yusef's bad luck was our gain. Two shots of antibiotics and he was cured. A charming man, he was active and efficient, and was with us for more than three years. We trusted him implicitly, and we allowed him to bring his wife, which meant endless children. Sadly he decided to open a coffee shop in Riyadh, and so we replaced him with Abdullah, our kitchen boy, who stayed with us for some time.

After two days in Rotterdam we boarded the ship, and, as she did not take passengers, we were assigned to the owner's cabin. Hasan was put in the sick bay, which was highly suitable, as he was sick for the entire voyage. On board we were amazed at the number of flowers in our cabin, as flowers were cheap and plentiful in Holland, so all our friends took advantage of this through Interflora. We were expected to eat with the ship's officers. The Captain was a splendid old man who had served in the German Navy throughout the war. The Mate was a young Prussian whose fair hair stood up on end like something out of *Struwwelpeter*. The Chief Engineer was a charming man whose wartime service was in German submarines. This clearly affected him. He was too partial to alcohol, and was replaced when the ship reached Genoa. We had a smooth run down the Channel, but woke up with a nasty shock when we rounded Cape Finisterre into mountainous seas. All the myriad vases of tulips and other flora finished up on the floor of the cabin as our steward arrived with a tray, which went the same way. The floor of our cabin was covered in flora, coffee, eggs and bacon. A glorious mixture! We went up to the deck, near the bridge, where we sat until the mess was cleared up.

Meals were rather difficult, as the officers liked to eat every variety of cold sausage, but we discovered that the ship was well supplied with German wine of an indifferent but quaffable variety. The ship's officers did not drink. This was to save money, so we were happy to share ours, so we paid for it at every meal. By reading Gibbon's *Decline and Fall of the Roman Empire*, I was able to escape the tedium of the voyage, and we soon reached Genoa, where we were scheduled to stay for the best part of two days. We had both been very unsteady on our feet after our rough passage, but we were able to board a train to San Remo, where we dined and gambled at the casino. We stopped at one point on the way when all the Italian passengers streamed across the tracks to visit an ice-cream seller on the other side. With much hooting, another train, eastbound, came down the track. The passengers leapt in all directions, but surprisingly escaped injury. When we left Genoa we were desperately hungry after the rigours of the voyage. The menu was entirely pasta of various kinds. On my query, the waiter recommended gnocchi.

Our journey through the Suez Canal and down the Red Sea was uncomfortably hot. Hasan was able to leave his cabin and join us for the last leg of the voyage. We cleared the Suez Canal, and finally disembarked at Jeddah. I had a stroke of good fortune, as one of my soldiers from Jordan, Mislem Museilem of the Harb Tribe, by then working for the Saudi Customs, was at the quayside when we arrived.

Recognition was happy and mutual. Mislem introduced me to the Director of Customs at Jeddah Port, and I explained that I had my shotgun with me. He agreed to keep it safely until I was able to arrange for its collection. Meanwhile our possessions were cleared, and he showed us to the Jeddah Palace Hotel, a run-down building normally used to house pilgrims during the Hajj pilgrimage. Hasan was left behind to accompany our belongings to Riyadh, to which we travelled by air.

We stayed for two days with the new British Ambassador, Colin Crowe, and his wife, in the old Embassy building on the seaward side of the old walled city. Humidity was high in the summer in Jeddah, and the Embassy air conditioners were large but inadequate. The Crowes were most hospitable. We appreciated our brief stay, but were glad to get away to dryer climes. After we settled in Riyadh, the following summer, we were very happy to be invited by the new Ambassador, Morgan Man, and his wife Patricia, who were extremely hospitable, and he was particularly kind in bringing my brandy in his pocket when he visited Riyadh.

At Riyadh we stayed at the Yemama Hotel. Yemama was the name of the village where, in an epic battle, Khalid bin Walid defeated Musaylimah al Kadhab, who had set himself up as a false prophet to rival the messenger of God.

The air-conditioning ducts were, in those days, inhabited by a colony of black rats, who were well fed by the guests due to their habit of bringing dates with them to the hotel. In the hotel, I met up with Kenneth Timbrell, now a local Brigadier, as one of our recommendations to the British Ministry of Defence was that local rank should be granted to the British Mission one up from their normal rank. The National Guard provided each of us with an estate car and a driver. Mine was Barak bin Moheimid Al Ataybi, the Brigadier's was also an Al Ataybi. Both drivers lived at Mahjuan on the eastern side of Riyadh, until Barak moved into our compound, as he was studying to be a police officer. Both became lifelong friends.

While we were in the lobby of the Yemama Hotel, a stranger came up and said to Pamela 'Are you married to Bromage?' She answered 'Yes,' at which point the stranger announced himself as Abdullah Behayan, and said that he had been the driver for Colonel Blackden, who had married Tannetta, of the Vesta family from the American colony. I never really discovered whether he knew us from when Hugh Blackden was in the Transjordan Frontier Force or whether it was later on when he joined the Arab Legion and commanded the 1st Regiment. He asked Pamela whether there was anything that she wanted from him. She told him that she was looking for accommodation in Riyadh, as we were promised air-conditioned accommodation when the British Mission was first established. Abdullah told her that he was a Hadhramy, and had worked for Mohamed bin Laden when the latter had organised the infrastructure of the new road network in the Kingdom. Whether he had a hand in real estate I never discovered, but she asked him to find a house for us. He found a house, just outside Riyadh, which belonged to a Shemary called Mohamed Abdullah

Alfahad, and which was just beside Al Mahroug, in which King Abdul Aziz had taken refuge when he recaptured Riyadh from the Shemary Governor in the 1890s. It was previously occupied by the son of one of the Emirs, who had left it in a somewhat dirty state. We looked around the house, saw that it had potential, and decided to rent it. It had high walls, large metal gates and opaque glass windows. No sooner were we in the house than my old friends from Jordan arrived consecutively on our door step. We ended up with 13 people within our walls. There was no rubbish collection, so we emptied our rubbish over the walls, and the goats could be seen devouring copies of the airmail *Times*!

In order to make it shipshape, Pamela co-opted the technicians from the British Aircraft Corporation – who were waiting in Riyadh to have their contracts signed – in exchange for lunches. They worked extremely well, removing the old paint left on the tiled floors, and generally making the house

The author's house at Riyadh.

habitable. We then asked the National Guard to take the house on our behalf.

We had some difficulties, as the local Bedouins, who by then had heard that the National Guard was renting the house, used to run wires off our mains to light their tents and, no doubt, refrigerators. Stealing or borrowing from the Government was not regarded as a crime in the way as it was from an individual, so we had a continuing problem over amateur electricians running wires off our mains, and we had to establish a patrol every day to see that our power lines were in order. I was amazed that no Bedouin was electrocuted, and all seemed to survive.

Abdullah Behayan had at least three sons. The eldest, Ibrahim, was a junior officer in the Saudi Army, and had an office not very far from the hotel. His second son was a qualified physician. Where he qualified I never found out, but I suspect that it was in Syria. We had a happy relationship with our new landlord. We owed a great deal to Abdullah Behayan for his kindness in arranging our accommodation.

We had to deal with a number of visitors from the United Kingdom who had managed to get hold of my name. We usually entertained them to lunch, and normally sent them back with a small bottle of alcohol, which they much appreciated. From time to time, the bootleggers turned up and rang the bell, with their lorry full of sheep, underneath which were crates of whisky.

We had to leave the children behind for a month with Nanny, in the care of my mother and Pamela's cousin,

The author's daughter with General Saleh Deham and Mehsin Mishel.

Nichola Colvin. This period turned into four months because the Yemama Hotel would not have been suitable for a two-month-old baby. In those days there were no direct telephone lines from Saudi Arabia to the United Kingdom, except via Paris. We prepared our house for Christmas, and the children and Nanny arrived in Beirut from London. They were met by the agent, Henri Heald. We did not recognise Nichola at all, because four months was a long time at her age.

When the Wakil for the National Guard called to wish us a happy Christmas, his driver brought into the drawing room a sack, out of which jumped two full-grown gazelle, one of which went straight through a lampshade.

The souk in Riyadh was remarkable for the range of objects available, offered as presents to Saudi princesses and passed on by their ladies-in-waiting to the merchants. There was a whole row of moneychangers, and one could bargain to get the cheapest rate on anything that you bought. Our driver, Barak, always accompanied Pamela when she was there. All shops closed at prayer time, and anyone unlucky enough to be inside had to wait until prayers were finished before they could leave.

Every Friday we used to take the children to the desert with a picnic. There were not many facilities open for them, except at Aramco, which made its pool available for their use, and they went every evening, enabling them to learn to swim at a very young age. There was only one English nanny. She worked for Adnan Khashoggi, an arms dealer, and his English wife, and looked after their daughter Nabeela.

At the headquarters of the National Guard (al Riasa) we were allotted a suite of three offices on the first floor, a short distance down the corridor from the Emir. An interpreter, Salim Baradi, had been appointed to the National Guard, and he shared our office, did our filing and translating, and was a huge asset to us. Salim is a Palestinian from Safad with a degree in Arabic literature from Damascus University. He was a schoolmaster at Mejma, home town of the Wakil,

The author's children at a picnic in the desert.

whose abilities had been recognised, leading to him being transferred to the National Guard. He is still in Riyadh forty years later, now retired, as a Saudi Arabian citizen with a grown-up family of intellectually able children. We had a coffee- and tea-maker assigned to us, as was customary in the National Guard, where the cost of tea and coffee made a significant dent in the budget, then 14,000 rials.

On the floor below us was the Wakil, his Office Director Amr, the General Director, Mohamed Al Aiban, and the various administrative offices which manned the guard.

Despite Crown Prince Faisal's initial poor impression of the Wakil, we found him to be an excellent manager, not afraid to take responsibility and able to cut repeated layers of entrenched bureaucracy, which were prevalent in Saudi Government departments at that time. The Wakil became an excellent Chief Executive for the Emir, who took command of the National Guard at the beginning of 1963 as his initial appointment. He proved to be a patient and shrewd commander with a dominant personality and formidable powers of leadership. King Faisal picked a winner when he selected him to command and reorganise the National Guard. The Emir was quick to recognise that Abdul Aziz Al Tuwaigary was an invaluable asset as the process of reorganisation got under way.

The Emir's palace in those days was in that zone of Riyadh known as Al Mraba. He held an evening *mejlis* at the palace every day of the week except Thursday. After dinner the business of the Guard and plans for the future were discussed. The regular attendants were the Wakil, the General Director, Ibrahim Al Husseini, Brigadier Timbrell and myself. Others wandered in. When one of the religious leaders, the Ulema, visited, the guard at the gate used to shout a warning. All cigarettes were extinguished and the ashtrays concealed under the carpet! Although smoking was frowned upon, it was widely practiced. The Emir himself used to smoke from time to time, but gradually gave up as his responsibilities increased. Once one of the Ulema sat on an ashtray under the carpet. Although the pious gentleman fidgeted slightly on his uncomfortable seat, he had the good manners not to notice, so the incident passed without comment. Several of the Emir's family used to visit to dine or talk. In the early days, there was no official deputy or stand-in for the Emir. When he was away, one of his brothers was co-opted to command the National Guard. I can remember Emir Abdul Majid standing in on one occasion. Later on, the appointment of Emir Bedr bin Abdul Aziz as deputy head of the National Guard ensured that a temporary replacement was always available. The Emir had a great sense of humour and fun, and was loyal to his subordinates. When a new General Director was recruited after the promotion of Mohamed Al Aiban, and was subsequently accused of some maladministration in his previous appointment, carrying the risk of imprisonment, the Emir pleaded his case and allowed him to retire on a pension. In those days the impediment in the Emir's speech was quite marked. He used it as an excuse to delay what came next, so he avoided any verbal gaffes. In time the impediment left him. He became a practised public speaker.

The National Guard headquarters was managed by civil servants. The military consisted of a uniformed element called *fedayin* and a tribal element called *mujahadin*, voluntary tribal levies under their own Sheikhs (Emirs). These were armed with small arms, and were the rough equivalent of our Territorial Army. They were often known as the White Army, due to their white clothing, and provided a readily accessible pool of extra manpower in the event of any external threat to the Kingdom. At that time the officers of the *fedayin* consisted of one Brigadier General, Ibrahim Al Rasheed, a Colonel Hamoud Sagran, a Lieutenant Colonel Ali Shuhaib, and a Major Menseh. All were retired from the Army. It was an inadequate nucleus on which to base a reorganisation. Ibrahim was a charming man without a strong personality, an advantage in a force at that time organised and managed by civil servants. The Rashida and his tribe are an offshoot of Huteim, which are numerous in the Arabian Gulf area. The Great Sheikh is Bin Barak in Central Nejd. They have no noble ancestry. No noble Bedouins will allow their daughters to marry into either tribe, although many of Huteimiat and Sherariat are exceptionally beautiful.

As I spent many years with the Jordanian Army, I was asked by the Rais to travel to Jordan with a view to persuading the Jordanian military authorities to release from their service any volunteers of Saudi Arabian origin who were prepared to join the Saudi Arabian National Guard. Major General Akash Al Zebn, Chief of Staff of the Jordan Armed Forces, was sympathetic and helpful. Some 22 experienced officers were transferred, and others followed. This influx of officers enabled two new *fedayin* units to be trained to basic standards, the National Guard School to be expanded, and officer training commenced, a development which turned out to be the foundation of the King Khalid Military Academy. The Rais's decision to bring officers of Saudi origin from Jordan was both timely and astute. Only two now remain in very senior positions, but the rest filled a vital gap, allowing time for officers from the National Guard to be selected and trained and to progress through the various stages of command to reach their present standards.

While all the re-organisation was taking place, the war between the Royalists and the Republicans in the Yemen intensified. The latter were reinforced by regular units of the Egyptian Army, some of which appeared to have threatened the borders of the Kingdom, south and east of Jizan and Nejran. The Guard shared the defence of the frontier with the Army. One *fedayin* unit and two *mujahadin* Alwi were deployed. D11 sets were sent to both areas, where the newly recruited operators received practical experience in the field far more effectively than in the classrooms of Umm Al Hammam. The set south of Jizan was machine gunned by an aircraft from the Yemen. Fortunately it missed the target. The decision to enlist the operators at the rank of sergeant major caused many problems later, and resulted in the some ill-informed criticism, but was justified by events. Without the operators, the communication network could not have been deployed. Back in Riyadh, Major General Obeid Al Khamash gave up command of the School in favour of Colonel Talab Fahad, and concentrated on the selection of potential officers for courses in the United States and Britain. Many of the present senior officers, both in the infantry and the signals, started their careers in the National Guard during this period.

The operations on the Yemen border were of great administrative value to the Guard. Before then, there was no experience of supplying troops in the field with food, arms, ammunition, petrol, medicines and medical equipment, nor was there a satisfactory system of distributing pay. All these evolved through trial and error: by the end of the first five years, the administrative and supply system was working satisfactorily.

At the headquarters, in Riasa, Ibrahim Al Husseini and his team were working on the plans for the establishment of a base at Khashm Al An. Plans were prepared and the first contracts were placed. In the beginning, when Prince Abdullah was first appointed, there were few camp buildings, garages and storage places for ammunition and equipment. Looking at the base at Khashm Al An now, it is truly amazing how much has been achieved in a comparatively few years.

The National Guard always kept a small administrative office in Jeddah. This was expanded from 1963. Mohamed Al Aiban was promoted from his post of Director General to become Wakil of the Western Region. This was the beginning of the expansion of the National Guard there. The Eastern region followed.

Finance limited the expansion of the Guard in the early years. Even taking into account the fall in the value of currencies all over the world, including Saudi Arabia, it is surprising to remember that in the beginning the spending power of the Rais was limited to 5000 riyals on any one project without the consent of the Council of Ministers, so the routine was prolonged, particularly during the summer, when the Court was at Taif.

The Rais and his staff worked day and night throughout the early period. The daily *mejlis* was attended by HRH, the two Wakils, the General Director and the two officers of the British Mission, at which plans were discussed, progress reported, and the various administrative difficulties resulting from a rapid deployment on the borders were ironed out.

Without the energy and leadership of the Prince, aided by Abdul Aziz Al Tuwaigary's detailed knowledge of the financial regulations of the Kingdom and his courage and flexibility in adapting them, success could never have been achieved. Even during the summer months, with the Court at Taif, Prince Abdullah kept in close contact with his staff and was informed of progress. He was truly the founding father of the National Guard, as we now know it.

General Hashim Said Hashim was the outgoing head of the Saudi Arabian Air Force, and became a lifelong friend of ours. When we returned to the United Kingdom, he regularly asked us to shoot with him, and we stayed at his house at Wickham in Berkshire. He was most generous and hospitable to us. On one occasion, a labrador belonging to one of the beaters peed on Harry Chapman Pincher's gun case, and when shouted at, turned round and peed on another one! Asma, his first wife, was the daughter of Abdullah Sulliman, Saudi Arabia's First Finance Minister. Sadly they parted, and he went on to marry the Turkish Ambassador's daughter and brought her for us to meet and vet. General Salah and I suggested to Hashim that he marry someone from a poorer family who would look after him in his old age. He lastly married a Syrian lady called Narriman. On the first night of their honeymoon, spent in our house, the lock slipped on their bedroom door and they were locked in. I had to extricate them with the aid of a screwdriver! We met many others who subsequently became friends, including Lois and Dick Viser, who were over from the United States and whom we used to see from time to time. They asked us to shoot in the United States on more than one occasion.

When we finally came to leave Saudi Arabia, we sold our possessions lock, stock and barrel to the First City Bank of New York, which was setting up an office there, and the National Guard transferred the tenancy to them, which meant that Pamela and the children could sleep in their beds until they left for the airport to catch the Boeing to Beirut which travelled at the King's discretion. They were lucky enough to be able to sit in the manager's air-conditioned office until the aircraft arrived, during which time I drove the car to Beirut, which took thirty hours, in order to be there to meet them and ship the car, so that it was there for our leave.

One of the problems that beset a family with young children in Saudi Arabia, was the difficulty of finding nannies who were prepared to live there. When we returned from the United Kingdom after a short period of leave, we employed a young nanny for our children. My mother suggested a suitable girl, but it soon turned out that she was happy to flirt, and Pamela discovered that she was on the pill. Obviously, the morals in Saudi Arabia varied considerably from those pertaining in the United Kingdom, so she was asked to leave.

During that period, a salesman called Geoffrey Edwards persuaded the Ministry of Defence to sell Lightning fighter aircraft to Saudi Arabia, as a result of which a large number of technicians from the British Aircraft Corporation descended on the Kingdom. Defence Sales, who were involved in pushing the sale of these aircrafts, acted independently of everything else that was happening between the United Kingdom and Saudi Arabia. I personally would not have advised the Saudis to buy this particular fighter aircraft, but that was none of my business. The Ministry of Defence regarded Defence Sales with some awe, and they overrode any such objections or difficulties which might have occurred along the way. Geoffrey Edwards was a clever salesman. In those days, as now, Defence Sales were considered to be most important to the UK's economy, and Geoffrey Edwards never failed to contact us when he was visiting from the United Kingdom, in case we had any needs.

Nannies, being few and far between, had become a magnet for those technicians who had not any specific employment at any particular time. I had engaged a replacement nanny from a mining family in Chesterfield. She was an excellent nanny in every way, but soon came under pressure. This was something of a personal embarrassment to me, as I had promised to look after her while she was in our service. She stayed with us until we returned to the United Kingdom, but she found life in London did not suit her, so went home to Chesterfield.

Our last three years in Saudi Arabia were extremely busy. I was in the office by 6.30 a.m., before the Emir arrived. He was not an early riser. I came back at two in the afternoon for lunch, and then off again to his *mejlis* every night, getting home about midnight. The Emir suffered from insomnia. Thursday night and all day Friday were my only days off. When he went hunting, we took some leave and went to Beirut to do our shopping. After we left Saudi Arabia, before one of his visits, he sent over Dr Shafat with Princess Sita, and asked Pamela to get her kitted out with clothes and find a nanny to go back to Saudi Arabia with her. Pamela duly found her clothes and interviewed nannies. One night we were woken up at about midnight by a call from the Emir asking Pamela to sack the nanny. She was duly paid off and told to leave, which meant that Pamela had to replace her immediately. Not an easy task. We found one of Pamela's cousins, Elizabeth Nall for the job. She lasted eighteen months! Not at all an easy job!

Quite a lot of Saudi Arabian princes were allowed four wives, which was in order according to Islamic law, provided that they were all treated alike. This meant that each wife was housed in a palace, and the prince would visit each in turn. Pamela used to visit the Emir's favourite wife, Princess Hussa al Shaalan while I was in the evening *mejlis*.

When we finally returned from Saudi Arabia, Pamela's uncle Bernard Cayzer thought we needed a break, and kindly took us to Montego Bay, and the following year to Antigua. When we were in Antigua we met Emma Sewell, the mother of Geoffrey Sewell, a brother officer of mine. She lived in a great house, and always wore a long muslin dress. We all played a great deal of bridge.

18

Tin: a Eulogy for an English Springer Spaniel

This is about the anniversary of Tin's death in Riyadh. Tin was an English springer spaniel who was sold to me by a certain Jack Chudley from Harpers Brooke kennels, near Kettering. He arrived just after I started my first term at the Staff College, which was then at Minley Manor, outside Camberley.

Max Graham telephoned me to say that he had rented a grouse moor from the Sinclair Estate at Thurso, for the duration of our holiday. The limit was 150 brace of grouse, which went with the three best beats on the Thurso River. Max also went on to say that we were to stay at Hallkirk, which is in the middle of the Thurso Estate. We agreed on the terms, and I collected Tin, who stayed with me at the Staff College for two nights before we left for Scotland in Max's car, an AC, rather a sporty model in those days. I made the mistake of putting Tin into the car the first night

Tin, the author's spaniel.

and, as it was not his car, he was terribly nervous and had squitters over the front seat, an inauspicious start to our journey. On our way to Scotland we travelled through Shap Fell, where I let Tin out, and he promptly flushed a covert of grouse, which he would do several times when we passed Shap Fell on future journeys.

Tin turned out to be an excellent retriever. On that first outing we shot a great many snipe and a few wild fowl in addition to our bag of grouse, but it was not until we returned to shoot at Azraq in Jordan that he showed his true worth.

Azraq is at the head water of the Wadi Sirhan, which divides Jordan from Saudi Arabia. There are two villages there, one settled by Druze, the other by Chechens. Tin used to come with us to Azraq in the back of the Land Rover. We would shoot sand grouse en route, and we shot the evening flight of duck when we arrived, and the morning flight the following day. Tin was invaluable, as he very rarely failed to pick up a bird. On one visit I invited a guest, the Commanding Office of the King's Dragoon Guards. When we were walking up snipe and he had shot one, he called to me rather plaintively, 'Nigel please bring your dog. I can't find the bird.' I brought Tin over, and he suddenly started to dig up the bog, and bits of mud and reed went flying. I became rather angry and cursed him, but along with all the debris that he unearthed came the corpse of the unfortunate snipe, which our guest had trodden into the bog. He was invaluable at Azraq, and an expert at marking birds which were shot. Clouds of teal and gargany used to pass overhead in the morning, and it was sometimes difficult to pick a bird without wounding others. Tin always picked his own bird first, and then started to search for ones that he reckoned were hit or wounded in some way, and these he pursued through the reeds and the rushes and the bog, and never, to my knowledge, left a wounded bird behind.

We used to travel to the south of the country to shoot chukar partridges. Early in the season, quail used to travel up from Egypt to southern Jordan, settling in the bean fields and other vegetation in the Jordan Valley. We had one incident when I was with a friend shooting quail among the broad beans. Pamela and his wife were happy to sit on the bank by the Land Rover. Suddenly two men approached, and attacked, and one of them grabbed her and started to strip off her clothes. I heard Pamela scream, so I swiftly returned and found the poor woman half-naked and in a state of shock, trying to cover herself with what was left of her clothing, the two men having run off. We, of course, reported this to the police. Subsequently, one of the mothers of the men came to me to help get her son out of police arrest, which I did, but the Embassy were furious that I had gone to the police behind their backs.

Another friend, Colonel Paddy Boden, from the 60th Rifle Regiment, used to come regularly to shoot quail, and we used to take it in turns to do the picnic. He always brought pizza pie, which we loathed. Pamela volunteered to provide picnics in the future, and all was well.

We used to stay outside Maan for the partridge shooting, which took place near Bir al Debaghat, in the Shera Mountains to the west. Tin was invaluable, but the rugged limestone of the Shera Mountains used to wear his poor feet to the quick, and he used to stay in his bed for a week to recover when we returned to Amman.

In those days a new Commander-in-Chief, Middle East, General Sir Roger Bower, was appointed, and he quickly became known as a very keen shot. Sir Charles Johnston, British Ambassador in Amman before he left us to become Governor of Aden, is a very erudite man with a fine wit, and he deputed me to be Chakari for the new Commander-in-Chief. All went well before his first visit, in which he wanted to shoot at Azraq. I took Tin with me, and I had hides built which were, I thought, in the right places for him shoot duck, but I did not reckon on the physique of the new Commander-in-Chief, who was extremely tall, measuring at least five foot from the base of his spine to the nape of his neck, and he stuck out from the hides I had built. During his first visit, I went out with Tin and lay on the mud flat about sixty yards from the Commander-in-Chief. The duck, seeing this monstrous figure, all turned left and passed over me, so I had a very successful shoot, but very few flew over the Commander-in-Chief, so my first task as a Chakari was a flop. Later on, when we were shooting quail in the Jordan Valley and the Ambassador was with us, Sir Roger used to borrow one of my guns. Every time a quail got up, all sycophantic Army officers like me shouted, 'Your bird, Sir Roger.' He did not miss very many, but on one occasion we were just about to go home when the last unfortunate quail flew up. The Ambassador, shouted 'Your Roger, Sir Bird.' Anyway, the great man went home happy, so Tin's duty was done.

I have never written a Eulogy for an English springer spaniel, but Tin certainly deserved one. In his later years he went with me to Saudi Arabia, where he became a well-known figure. When he became ill, King Abdullah bin Abdul Aziz lent me a veterinary surgeon to see if there was anything that could be done to help him, but he died a natural death in Riyadh from kidney failure and longevity. He was then nearly 14 years old.

During his life he went twice to the quarantine kennels at Hackbridge, where he was in quarantine on my return from the Middle East. On one of these visits Pamela brought him some jam tarts which she found on our way to the kennels, and she said to the girl selling the jam tarts, 'I hope these will do for my for spaniel.' She was furious.

Tinny was a very intelligent spaniel. When I was living in the mess in Zirqa, he sometimes came into my bed, but when I got engaged to Pamela she said no dogs in beds or on the furniture. This did not suit Tinny, so when we were out, he always managed to pull back the bed cover and get in and put his head on the pillow. When we returned he was always at the top of the stairs wagging his tail. When we went to bed we could see where he had been, as he had been unable to pull back to cover, and the pillow was warm!

19

Service Attachés' and Advisers' Section (SAAS), Ministry of Defence, 1966

In London I was appointed to the Service Attachés' and Advisers' Section in the Ministry of Defence. The duties involved visiting various military attachés and advisers to look at their establishments and to recommend to them any changes that might be needed. I can remember in the case of Sierra Leone I disestablished a whole ship belonging to the Royal Navy which, for some reason, had been allowed to remain there without any obvious purpose. I also visited the Defence Attaché at Lagos, who had been involved in some difficulty over his relations with the Nigerians there. I stayed with the Military Attaché for a day or two, and he kindly lent me his car and driver to go and visit the area. I duly went, and was impressed by the number of young ladies who tried to stop the car, presumably in the likelihood of being picked up for sexual relations. The figures of these nubile young Nigerians were quite elegant, but they should have known better than to impose themselves on a travelling diplomat.

Another visit took me to Peking (Beijing), where I had to walk across a bridge into China. At that time, the only way into China was to walk over the bridge, carrying your own suitcase.

Once, when I was Captain of the week, Colonel John Weston Simons, Defence Attaché in Peking, died suddenly. I had to make the necessary arrangements to repatriate his body in the middle of the night and inform his family.

At the end of my posting to the Service Attachés' and Advisers' Section in the Ministry of Defence, I lobbied the office of the Military Attaché in London District for a good appointment as Lt Colonel.

20

Kuwait, 1968

I was assigned to the Kuwait Liaison Team. I knew nothing about Kuwait, except that it had become one of the richest of the Gulf States. It was rumoured that when King Abdul Aziz of Saudi Arabia visited Sheikh Mubarak, the then ruler of Kuwait, the King said to the Sheikh, 'You have very little land, but I will see what more I can give you. You had better have that piece.' Waving his hand, he delineated the border outside Kuwait, which turned out to be one of the most prolific oil fields that were the font of the Kuwait Government's riches. Kuwait had hitherto been a minor player in the Gulf region. Although many Kuwaitis were charming as individuals, some of them were awful parvenus.

Pamela and I were given a nice house by the seashore, in the area of Kuwait known as Salmiya, where we ensconced our servant Abdullah, who had accompanied us from London,

A family photograph taken at 56 Ladbroke Grove, preceding al Kuwait.

to look after us. I found the Kuwaitis were obsessed with their new riches. They regarded all newcomers in their state as serfs, and treated them accordingly.

One of the duties of the Kuwait Liaison Team was to draw up plans for the defence of the city. The only road out of Kuwait, to the north, went up an incline to the Mutla Ridge. After Kuwait was invaded by Iraq, while we were in Jordan, many of the invaders were trapped on the road leading to the high ground, but that was in the future, and at that stage any invasion of Kuwait was a mere possibility. In Kuwait City itself, I found the inhabitants to be as charming as Arabs are.

A number of Bedouins from various tribes across Arabia settled in Kuwait, presumably because of money. These Bedouins formed the police and security forces of the Gulf states, but the Kuwaitis did not allow their citizenship to be passed out of their hands, and as a result the Bedouin tribesmen were treated as outcasts and were given the title of Bidun (meaning 'without'). I argued against this policy, at length, but did not get very far in changing the Kuwaiti outlook. Because of their arrogance, the Kuwaitis were unable to defend themselves as they had no Army and no Police of their own to do so; they surrendered to the Iraqis very quickly.

We took a taxi from Tehran to Abdeli. When we were climbing the mountain, the driver started to turn the corners at great speed, and was obviously trying to frighten us, so I told him he had to go faster and be more in control of his car, at which point he slowed down and we proceeded at a sensible pace.

When the house was ready, Nanny put our daughter Nichola on an aeroplane at Heathrow, in the care of an air-hostess as she was only six years old. She went to the Army School, and I dropped her each morning on the way to work and picked her up on my return.

Our son Charles was at his prep school, and came to visit us during the school holidays. He had learnt to water-ski in Beirut, and was able to follow our boat on his skis. It was typical of the Kuwaiti arrogance that while the children were waterskiing, they ran their launches very close in order to give us all a fright, which they did out of sheer devilment.

We had a washing lady who was called Mary Mother of Jesus (Um Easa). She came in with the news that Nasr was dead, and Pamela remarked, 'Thank God for that,' and I reposted 'God have mercy on him.'

My next appointment was to attend the Intelligence and Security course at Maresfield in preparation for my next appointment as Defence Attaché in the Gulf. Having sold 56 Ladbroke Grove, we had to have an Army quarter, and all that was available was a Captain's quarter at 49 Coldstream Gardens, Putney, which was a wooden house and only had one bathroom, which sadly meant parting with Abdullah, our Yemeni help. After one leave I returned to Coldstream Gardens to find that the deep freeze in the garage gave out a nasty smell, and discovered a mass of maggots when I opened the door, and which I had to clear up.

My mother and Pamela's grandmother died within a month of each other, and the spare year helped us to get Barland House straight. Barland House had originally been a hunting box for King Charles I, who fled there after the Battle of Naseby. All during that year we lived in the flat which we had turned into habitable accommodation from a deep-litter chicken run. We then let it to the RSPB when we moved properly into Barland House. At the same time, we rebuilt Upper Stocken and Lower Stocken cottages and let them to the RSPB. Pamela used to stay at Barland House in the school holidays, and I took leave when I could.

The following year would have been for an Arabic course, in preparation for my post as Defence Attaché to the Emirates, but because I was already fluent in Arabic I was excused, which gave us a year to settle in and sort out the garden.

21

The Emirates, 1976–78

I was appointed Defence Attaché to the United Arab Emirates, where we were given a small villa at Jumeirah in Dubai, almost on the beach. We had one week in great heat to unpack and clean up before our children arrived. We worked night and day. My predecessor had not cleaned up the builder's debris when he had handed over the villa. Every time we touched a tap we received a mild electric shock! I reported this to London, and the Foreign Office sent out an inspector to look at our facilities. When the inspector arrived, he grabbed a tap and got the necessary shock. Help was very difficult to find, but we found an Indian named Omal, who was not exactly honest.

On our arrival, we were put into the most dreadful, primitive hotel by our staff sergeant, from which we were luckily and quickly moved and where we met Rosanne Lowe, whose children had just gone to school. She was very unhappy, so Pamela put an end to it by telling her that they must get on and do some work, which was the start of a shop in the middle of the desert called Pictures and Presents, which was much needed by the expatriots. Every Christmas Pamela and Rosanne went around the seven emirates visiting the hospitals, so that any British doctors and nurses could buy British Christmas cards and presents for their families. We packed as much as we could into Rosanne's Land Rover. We could not use our staff car or our car as they had diplomatic number plates. This service became very popular. We had one two-day exhibition in Ras al Khaimah, and stayed with friends for two nights. The shop shut during the school holidays. It was great fun, and a success.

Admiral Sir Charles Madden and Lady Madden came out to Dubai to have an exhibition of his watercolours, at Pictures and Presents. Sir Charles was a great help in buying the David Roberts lithographs of the Middle East and all the maps and various watercolours. We were lucky to find a very good local framer. The shop flourished, but Pamela and I had to fly to Shiraz three months before the coup which overthrew the Shah. The atmosphere was very uneasy. The reason we had gone was because the Hilton could not liberate its pictures from Customs, and needed hangings and rugs to make up for them, which we were able to find for them.

One night when I went to fetch Pamela from the shop it was dark and she was standing by the Range Rover and she became squashed between the Volvo and the Land Rover and cracked her pelvis. She had to go off to the local hospital to be x-rayed, and had to spend the night there. It was just like a farmyard, with all the patients screaming. The next day we moved her to a private room for one night. My staff sergeant and I carried her out, and we took her home, where she had to lie on her back for a month. We were lucky enough to find two English nurses who came in on their way to and from work to make Pamela comfortable. The Ministry of Defence decided that it was cheaper to pay the nurses than to fly her home. It was a month before she could move, and it was the start of Christmas holidays and the children were due out. For a month, Pamela was lying flat on her back in bed with a broken pelvis. The kitchen boy used to bring her a tray with kitchen implements and ingredients on it, from which she managed to make, for example, soufflés with neat paper collars and also starters and savouries for all the dinners. Our daughter, who was aged 14, stood in for Pamela and acted as hostess at the dinners. There was no alternative as the entertaining had to carry on.

On our departure, we telephoned the manager of Steel Brothers to ask if they would like to take on our agencies and buy our remaining stock, which they willingly did.

One of the duties of the Defence Attaché was to travel around the various emirates. Three times a week I went to Abu Dhabi in a car without air conditioning. On one visit to Um al Quwain the son of the Ruler took us out in a boat called a cigarette, which was very frightening as he did not take his boatman, who knew how to drive it. We were nearly vertical, and had to hang on for our lives.

Ships' visits involved meeting, entertaining and seeing off the Navy. I remember the visit of Admiral Sir Henry Leach, the First Sea Lord. His Flag Officer had to share a bathroom with him, and they had to use our children's bedrooms.

After one ship's visit, we went to Oman to stay with the Ambassador, Jim Treadwell. I was not able to go until the last night, when Peter Thwaits, a Grenadier, gave a large dinner for me on my arrival. Our son, Charles, took our car two hundred miles across the desert, with Pamela and Nichola and our driver.

The climate was dreadful. It was desperately hot and humid. It was so humid that our two central air conditioners produced twenty-four gallons of distilled water every day. Spring holidays were the best time of year, climate-wise, for our children to visit. We were very relieved when our tour ended.

On our return, we were asked to host Sheikh Mohamed bin Rashid of Dubai for the Government luncheon at Ascot Week. It poured with rain the whole time, and Sheikh Mohamed went to the paddock before each race, accompanied by Pamela. He even declined tea with the Queen Mother because his horse was running in the next race!

My life in Arabia was not finished, as I became a consultant to Prince Abdullah bin Abdul Aziz, in his role as Head of the National Guard. This necessitated my return to Saudi Arabia for a fortnight twice a year for many years.

22

Consultancies, 1978

Once I had retired from my active life in Arabia, I started work as a consultant for various firms.

The first was British Caledonian Airways, which was then based in London. The reward for that particular consultancy was that I was to be given first-class tickets to Hong Kong and accommodation for four people. On the strength of getting the airline the route to Saudi Arabia, we took our friends Sir Edward and Lady Hulse as our guests and travelled to Hong Kong, Bangkok and China.

Next, was Marsh McLennan, the well-known insurance brokerage firm. Captain Martin Busk, who was representing Marsh McLennan, invited himself to come with me when I next went out to Saudi Arabia. I particularly told Martin that on no account was he to take a camera with him, but he clearly thought otherwise. Shortly after we arrived in Riyadh, he produced his camera and started photographing a signpost

The author at a feast given in his honour.

at a road junction. He was immediately picked up by the police, who arrested him. I intervened and bargained with the police. As a result I exchanged the camera for Captain Busk! This was very satisfactory, as the moment he returned to the United Kingdom he claimed on his insurance policy for another camera, a somewhat newer model than the one he had handed over.

Another consultancy was with Helical Bar, which provided steel for the construction industry. This post lasted for some years. I remember taking the chairman, Laurence Kelly, with me on one of my trips to Jeddah.

My main consultancy was with Prince (now King) Abdullah bin Abdul Aziz. I looked after his children when they came to the United Kingdom, and kept them out of mischief. One of my responsibilities was to overview the office in London, which entailed my visiting every day. That came to an end when one of the King's relations, who was doing the same job in Washington, was involved in some financial scandal, as a result of which the King closed the offices in London and Washington simultaneously, at which point my official consultancy ended, but I remained free to visit Saudi Arabia and Jordan as an unofficial visitor.

On our first return to Jordan in the late 1980s we no sooner landed and arrived at our hotel than a message came from the Royal Palace to say that a car was on its way to collect me. I hurriedly donned a suit and jumped into the car. King Hussein was there waiting for me, and we sat and chatted for quite some time, having tea and coffee, and he put at my disposal a driver, a car, a helicopter and anything else that I should need. There were numerous dinners to attend, and Abu Hashim (Head of the Bardia Police) gave a lunch for us. Sadly the day on which we went to Aqaba the weather was very foggy, and we could not go by helicopter so we drove, calling in at the new hotel at Petra. In Aqaba we were able to visit some of Radwan's family. The Mayor of Amman, Lafi Hareithan, gave a lunch for us. General Fuaz Maher, a Circassian, entertained us. We met many of our old friends, including Isa Qsus, who had been my signal's officer, and who gave us dinner and still telephones us each Christmas to wish us well.

In 1999 when I was on en route to such a visit, I heard a wireless broadcast that King Hussein had died on 7 February. I made arrangements to change aircraft immediately, and flew directly to Amman, where I was able to join the procession following the King's coffin to the Royal Cemetery at Jebal Amman for burial.

In October 2007, shortly after King Abdullah was raised to the throne of Saudi Arabia, he paid a state visit to London in October. Pamela and I were invited to attend the State Banquet at Buckingham Palace. While waiting to shake hands with the Queen and the Duke of Edinburgh, King Abdullah boomed out, 'Bromage!' Her Majesty the Queen was delighted that he had found a long-standing friend, and I was able to chat with him and the Duke of Edinburgh.

In 2010 the Saudi British Society nominated me for their Rawabi Holding Award for lifetime services to Great Britain and the Kingdom of Saudi Arabia, given by the Abdul Aziz al Turki Charitable Foundation.

I have often been asked which of the Arab countries in which I have served I liked most. My answer to that would be in the first instance Jordan, where I started my life in Arabia, and where I still have very many friends. Jordan is a happy country where the people support their monarchy and there has never been a serious attempt at a revolution, apart from that of Ali Abu Nuwar. The second country is Saudi Arabia. I have many friends in the Kingdom, many of whom are very dear to me. Abdul Aziz Al Tuwaigary was one of them, and General Saleh Deham another, among many. Our telephone rings often, wishing us good health and asking after ourselves and our children since we left. I find the people of both countries charming and agreeable, and all that we have known have been good friends. On the occasions on which we have returned, we have been entertained liberally, and in the case of the funeral of King Hussein, it was with great sadness that I saw his coffin carried to the Royal Cemetery.

Appendix:
Personalities

King Abdullah bin Hussein was a man of great intellect. He had been brought up in the Court at Istanbul, where Eastern and Western political thought were both in evidence, at the end of the nineteenth century. He was deep-thinking, pragmatic and far in advance, both in intellect and experience, of all the members of his Cabinet; indeed of others in the Arab League who were directly involved in the war with the Israelis. Unfortunately, there was a deep dynastic enmity between the Hashimites, who had only been evicted from the Hejaz thirty years before, and the House of Saud. King Abdullah was a man of forceful personality. He was outspoken, did not suffer fools gladly, and was easily angered. He hated losing at chess.

Talal bin Hussein used to suffer from brainstorms, and at one point chased his Prime Minister all the way to Salt and Jericho, where he took refuge in the Royal Palace at Shunah. He only lasted a short time, as he was mentally unstable, and he was forced to transfer the kingship to his son, Hussein.

King Hussein bin Talal was outstanding among Middle Eastern monarchs of his time. He was educated at Harrow, followed by Sandhurst. He learnt to fly, and was an able pilot. He was married to an Egyptian, Sharifa Dina bint Abdul-Hamid, who was university educated, and he was very much her junior. Sadly the marriage did not last. They had one daughter. Secondly, he married Princess Muna, who was the daughter of a Royal Engineer stationed at Amman. They lived happily in the Palace at Shuneh for ten years and had four children, one of whom is the present King. Thirdly, he married Alia, by whom he had two children, and they adopted a third. This was his happiest marriage, but sadly she died in a helicopter accident and left him broken-hearted. His last marriage was to Lisa Halaby, who was half Lebanese and half American, and became Queen Noor. They had four children. They remained married until his death.

King Abdullah bin Hussein was appointed Crown Prince on King Hussein's deathbed, and is the current King. He is married to Queen Rania of Palestinian parentage. She works extremely hard for various charities.

Sir John Bagot Glubb (Glubb Pasha) was a man of enormous intellect and ability, but with little previous experience as a High Commander in battle. He had remarkable patience, and was able to pick his way through the political and military minefield that existed during those troubled times. He had the ability to know and anticipate Arab politicians' thinking. He carried the weight of Transjordan's wars against the Israelis on his shoulders, and should be given credit for their success. After his death in 1986, King Hussein gave the address at his memorial service in London.

General Habis al Majali came from an important family from Kerak. He was the Jordanian Commander who defeated the Israeli attack on the Jordanian positions outside Yalu. He was fêted as a hero by the Jordanians, and went on to be the Chief of Staff of the Jordanian Armed Forces.

General Saleh Deham al Shemary came to me in Jordan, where he had joined the Arab Legion at the age of 15, because of his physique: he was a strapping young man, and was accepted without query to his age, as Bedouins never know their date of birth. He has remained a very close friend, and speaks to us on the telephone regularly. He soldiered on, and being able, he moved up through the ranks to become a Major General and subsequently became ADC to the Crown Prince, now King.

Brigadier-General Mohamed Hashim al Jundi came over from the Hijaz with Glubb Pasha, and was head of the Badia Police, who were the Desert Police force in Jordan. He owned the house we rented at Azraq, which he let to me. He exercised strict control over his police, who had stations all over Jordan. He was well respected, and during my time in Jordan the Desert Police, who were stationed from Irbid in the north to Maan and Aqaba in the south, were always well equipped and prepared, in the later stages, to help with the tourist industry, which increased remarkably with the years. He retired after an exemplary career, soon after Glubb Pasha.

Count Folke Bernadotte was an intelligent and charming aristocrat who was determined to be scrupulously impartial and was, in my opinion, a thoroughly good man.

King Saud bin Abdullah bin Abdul Aziz was King of Saudi Arabia between 1953 and 1964 when he abdicated because of ill-health.

King Faisal bin Abdul Aziz al Saud was King of Saudi Arabia between 1964 and 1975, when he was assassinated by his nephew.

King Abdullah bin Abdul Aziz is a good King with a powerful personality. Previously, he was the Commander of the National Guard from 1963 until he became King.

Abdullah Behayan was a Hadramy employed by Mohamed Bin Laden when he was building an infrastructure of metal roads in the Kingdom of Saudi Arabia, and who helped my wife, Pamela, to secure a good house at al Mahroug near Riyadh.

Michael Colvin was in the Grenadier Guards on a short-term commission. After leaving the Regiment he eventually became a member of parliament for Romsey in Hampshire. He was a very talented artist and copyist.

Sir Charles Johnston was the British Ambassador to Jordan between 1956 and 1959. He married Natasha Begratzien, a member of the Ruling Family of Georgia, whose mother subsequently became Abbess of the Russian Convent in Jerusalem. On his retirement, he translated Pushkin's novel in verse, *Eugene Onegin*, and Lermontov from Russian.

Theo Larsen was a Swedish businessman who represented Contraves AG, the Swiss arms dealer, and he used to stay with us regularly when we were in Riyadh.

Sir Michael Dylwyn-Venables-Llewellyn, an ex-Grenadier, had been the owner of Barland House in Radnorshire, and had split the estate into two halves during the Second World War. He lived there while his father was still alive, and then moved to the family estate at Newbridge-on-Wye.

Kim Philby was the well-known spy.

Dame Freya Stark was born in Paris in 1893. She became an archaeologist and travel writer, and eventually married Stuart Perowne, a homosexual. She died in Italy at the age of 100.

Index